Keeping Your Heart
The Key to Walking with God

Allan Lewis

Copyright © 2021, Allan Lewis

No part of this publication may be reproduced or transmitted in any form or by any means, electronic or mechanical, including photocopying and recording, or by any information storage and retrieval system, except in the case of brief quotations for use in articles and reviews, without written permission from the copyright owner.

The views expressed in the book are the author's and do not necessarily reflect those of the publisher.

Cover Design: http://HarvestCreek.net

Editing: David Yeazell; Yeazell Consulting, P.O. Box 383194, Duncanville, TX 75138; 817-456-9267; info@yeazellconsulting.com

Scripture references are the King James Version of the Holy Bible unless otherwise noted.

7710-T Cherry Park Dr, Ste 224
Houston, TX 77095
www.WorldwidePublishingGroup.com
(713) 766-4271

ISBN: 978-1-64830-434-7

What Others Are Saying

"As a practicing Doctor of Chiropractic for more than forty-six years, who works with the Law of Nature which God has prescribed to all people, I endorse Allan Lewis's book, *Keeping the Heart*. I personally and professionally use these principles and have clinically observed patients attaining a heightened level of health restoration."

– **Dr. Curtis Kannegieter, D.C.**

"The teaching in this book, *Keeping the Heart*, changed my life. Read it, receive, and apply it, and it will change yours too."

– **Donna Lynn**

"This tremendous series *Keeping the Heart, The Key to Walking with God* is one of the most revelatory teachings on the inner workings of the soul I have heard. Within these pages are the keys that will unlock the inner depths of the mind, will, and emotions. I strongly encourage every believer, whether new to the faith or mature in the Lord to delve into the depths of these teachings and have your soul refreshed and your heart renewed."

– **Pastor Dave Thompson** – Senior Pastor, *Gateway on Mt. Zion*

"There is a wealth of Godly wisdom contained in Pastor Al Lewis' book, *Keeping the Heart*. In it, you will find the keys to walking intimately with the Father. This book will equip and inspire you and deepen your relationship with God."

– **Joe Vendegnia**, Dean of *Headwaters Bible Institute, Gateway on Mount Zion Church,* Golden, Colorado

"It's my honor and privilege to know Allan Lewis and to understand his poignant truths about the heart and how to apply the simple gospel to what God describes as guarding and protecting your heart. In this book, he explains how to rid one's heart of fear and brokenness; and how to restore and renew it with the Word of God.

His humor and whimsical correlations equating the heart to the production room in a sound studio are brilliant. The heart is the main production room for the whole body. If the heart is healthy all is well. If it is malfunctioning, the sirens go off. Allan explains the heart, the identity, and authority of godly fatherhood, and how it can be achieved.

If you hunger for righteousness, freedom, and healed heart, this book is for you. Thank you, Allan Lewis for sharing your father's heart with me, you have equipped me to reach new levels in Christ."

– **Geralyn Pomponio**, Deacon, *Gateway on Mt. Zion Church*,
Golden, Colorado

"I just finished the *Keeping the Heart* series. It was so amazing! I needed it right now to understand God's process in me. It helped bring the peace I needed. Thank you!"

– **Katie Steenburgh**

Contents

Acknowledgments 1

Introduction 3

Chapter 1: What is the Heart? 5

Chapter 2: The Fixed and Established Heart 16

Chapter 3: How to Have a "Want to" Heart 26

Chapter 4: How to Get Christ Back on the Throne of Your Heart 37

Chapter 5: How to Have a Pure Heart 53

Chapter 6: How to Keep your Heart 63

Chapter 7: Axing the Roots 75

Chapter 8: Seeds in the Heart 89

Chapter 9: If Your Heart Does Not Condemn You 102

Chapter 10: Sanctify God in Your Hearts 111

Chapter 11: Results of Sanctifying God in Your Heart 124

Conclusion 138

Acknowledgments

First, I thank my precious wife, Marlyce, who awaits me in heaven. She was my closest friend, constant companion, encourager, intercessor, and editor. Without her at my side, this book may have never been published. She was always a prayer warrior for me as I studied and then presented, in sermon form, the messages that the Lord Jesus had given me through the Holy Spirit.

Secondly, I acknowledge Gloria Hollard, who took all the recorded sermons I delivered on the heart and transcribed them into a readable format. The tremendous number of hours involved in this significant project is beyond imagination. Thank you, Gloria, for being such an excellent servant of the Lord Jesus.

Thirdly, to Shawn Sturm—my son in the Lord—for his work to format my words into a workable print-ready format. Thank you, Shawn.

Fourthly, to my son Butch for his persistence in getting me to "get the book finished". He has been a great encouragement to me and has been responsible for getting the printing accomplished. Thank you.

Good proofreaders are a necessity. My daughter-in-law Cami has provided an excellent service in that area. Thank you, Cami.

I would be amiss if I did not include all the members of my congregation, Cathedral of the Rockies. They were a wonderful group of sponges that soaked up all the Word that I could deliver. They were a great group to pastor, and I want to acknowledge them for all the great encouragement they gave and continue to give. Bless you.

I was given a word at a Sunday night service while standing expectantly in a prayer line. The guest speaker that night was Chris Hill (Bishop T.D. Jakes' former youth pastor). As Chris came down the prayer line, he laid his hands on me, leaned over, and said, "I see libraries in you." That word was a great blessing to me—this book is just the first of many inside me waiting to get out.

Introduction

I believe this book will be somewhat different from others that you have read. This may sound like an extremist statement, but I encourage you to read all the way through and see if it is not a challenge to you as it has been to many others. It is my desire to stimulate you and the life you wish to live in God. As you read, I desire that you examine your life in light of the Word of God in a way that you may not have previously considered. If you decide to activate the principles that you read, I believe you will find many problems answered which have "bugged" or tormented you for some time. The questions that have arisen from Romans 7— *"The things I do not want to do, I do; and the things I want to do, I do not…"*—will become clearer to you after you read this book AND begin to practice the truths found herein. It will not only provide answers to questions you may have had, but it will give revelation on a subject that is prolific but very misunderstood. In my ministry, I have seen tremendous changes in the lives of people after they applied the principles you are about to discover.

The heart is a common word and a familiar topic to all of us who have named the name of Jesus. But I believe that the full impact the Holy Spirit intended on this subject has eluded us. Having been trained to believe the heart was to be viewed in a particular way, I was surprisingly shocked to see that the real meaning was different. It was at that point I began to understand the significant depths we had missed. As I explored the Greek and Hebrew texts, I began to see a type of road map develop that I believe the Holy Spirit wants us to travel. It is a map with clear direction and clear signposts along the way that will keep us on course and allow us to see why the diversions and distractions are ever-present. When we do not see the significance and absolute importance a spiritual truth plays in our walk in the Spirit, we will not fulfill the personal destiny Father God has carefully established for each one of us. I believe the knowledge and understanding of the heart will open doors of that destiny for you that would be difficult to ascertain any other way. This study has changed my ministry, and I pray it will have a dramatic impact on you. So, read on with great anticipation, and let us begin our journey together with great hope and expectation. I bless you as you journey through the knowledge of the heart.

Chapter 1

What is the Heart?

The subject of the heart is **the key** to many of the problems that we face as human beings. Without a proper understanding of the heart and how it operates, we do not have a foundation on which to base our belief system. In the following pages, I want to share with you what the Holy Spirit has shown me as I have studied the Word of God. A proper understanding of the heart is essential for much that we face in life—assisting us with solutions to everyday situations, problems, and questions—situations that many people have stumbled over, and due to a lack of understanding, have dismissed God out of. As we journey through these pages, I hope you will take a second look at any problems you are encountering and begin to view those problems considering this new understanding of the heart: **the key** to walking with God.

In the church, we often sing the words: "Into my heart, into my heart, come into my heart Lord Jesus." We make invitations and encourage people to invite Jesus into their hearts. Thank God for the people who have come to Christ through those altar calls. But do we really understand what is being said? What picture or image are we establishing? Is it a correct image? If we are going to develop spiritually and be conformed to the image of Christ, then we must come into an understanding of the heart—what it is and how it operates.

During the early years of my spiritual development, I was taught that the heart and spirit are one and the same. As I began to study for myself and dig into the Hebrew and Greek definitions of the terms, the concept of heart and spirit being synonymous was very unsettling to me because many verses in the Bible were seemingly contrary to that teaching. So, I concluded that there must be a difference between the heart and the spirit.

As I researched and studied, I began to teach that there are two parts to the heart: the soul and the spirit. But, upon further study, I discovered that I did not see it correctly. Hebrews 3:12 says: *"Take heed brethren lest there be in any of you an evil heart of unbelief, in departing from the living God."* If heart and spirit are the same, then how could evil co-exist with the life of God in the born-again human spirit? If the definition of heart meant spirit and soul, then how could the heart be called evil? I then discovered Jeremiah 17:9: *"The heart is deceitful above all things, and desperately wicked; who can know it?"* Now I really had a conflict if heart and spirit are synonymous.

Genesis 1:26 tells us that God (Elohim—plural for God) said: "… *Let us make man in our image, after our likeness*…." As I studied further, I eventually came to the realization that in order to fully understand *"in our image and after our likeness,"* we must understand the essence of God. In John 4, Jesus had a conversation with the woman at the well. In that discourse, Jesus said that God is a **Spirit.** Consider this, if God is a spirit and we are made in His image and likeness, then that makes us a spirit also. If heart and spirit are synonymous, then how could something made in the image (exact duplication in-kind) and likeness of God be *"deceitful above all things"*?

Since I didn't believe the likeness of God could be deceitful, I, therefore, concluded that the heart and spirit must be separate and different. If they are separate and different, then surely sin could pollute and contaminate one and not the other. Genesis 2:7 states that God breathed in the nostrils of man, and man became a living soul. Do you see the order? The spirit, made in the image and likeness of God, gave life to the soul. The soul was the part of us that sinned and thus brought death. The soul area is that part of us that houses the heart, and as a result, it can be (before Jesus comes in) deceitful above all things.

Thank God the Bible is not vague and certainly not contradictory in what it teaches. Our Father, through His Word, gives us a clear understanding of a very crucial subject. We may have to dig into the text and pray and meditate on it to get to the real meaning, but we have the assurance that our digging is not in vain as the Holy Spirit has a mandate from our Father to "lead and guide us into *all* truth."

It is important that we realize that the heart and the spirit are not and could not be equivalent or synonymous because too many verses in the Bible contradict that premise. If you are like me, you have read those verses multiple times, passing over them and saying, "I guess I do not understand that." I want to move you beyond misunderstanding into a clear understanding of the heart.

So, what we need to do is to approach this study from a very realistic viewpoint. Isaiah 28:9-10 states that *"Whom shall He teach knowledge? And whom shall He make to understand doctrine? Them that are weaned from the milk, and drawn from the breasts. For precept must be upon precept; precept upon precept; line upon line, line upon line; here a little, and there a little."*

That is the principle of how we will study the subject of THE heart—learning and growing in the things of God starting with precept upon precept; line upon line; here a little, there a little.

What is the Heart?

The heart is the **seat** (or authority) of the senses, the emotions, the will, and the intellect. The heart is part of the soul but is not all of the soul. The heart is the authority of the soul or the very being of a man. We have been taught that the soul is the mind, will, emotions, and intellect. But the soul is their locale, not their origination. So, if we can accept this definition, then the question is: where do those emotions, will, and senses come from? They are not nebulous things somewhere in our soul. There must be a place from where they originate within a person. I propose to you that the place where they originate is the heart.

Let me state it again: the heart is the **seat**, the **authority**, the place of **origination** of the emotions, the senses, the mind, the will, and the intellect. It's the central origination point. So, the heart is housed within the soul, but it is not the same as the soul. It is not the totality of the soul but rather the central focal point of the soul.

The heart is the production place or the production room for the emotions, the will, the senses, and the intellect. If you're producing or recording an album of songs, you do that in a studio where the necessary recording and production equipment is housed. In the production room, the instrumental music is recorded as well as the vocals. Sound is mixed there, splicing and dubbing, and all technical work is done in the production room where the equipment is located. All the production is done within the studio. The studio is self-sufficient for producing a record album. The final output (record/CD) is what we get and enjoy.

In a recording studio, there are two parts. One area is where the performer is located. That area is where the instruments and vocals are contained. This area is also where all the microphones are used. The second part of the studio is the control board with all the recording, mixing, and receiving equipment. Separating the two sections is a thick pane of glass that allows either side to see each other without hearing the sounds from the other side. I equate the heart to the control-recording board with all its instrumentation and wonderful mixing ability. But a problem exists in that you may have the greatest musicians on one side of the glass that can produce the finest sounds known to man, but, if the instrument board on the other side of the glass is faulty in any way, the sound produced on the musician side will not be produced properly. Consequently, the result will be faulty and not pleasing at all. So it is with the heart. The input may be great (sermons, music, etc.), but if the heart has some "short circuits," then the results will be much less than desired. If the control board (the heart) is not in proper working order, then the result will be ugly. So, if we can get the control board clean and have all the circuits working properly, we can then expect the outcome to be in keeping with what was originally desired. That process is what we will discuss in the following chapters.

The heart includes not only the emotions, senses, will, and intellect, but it also includes the desires, the passions, and the appetites—the heart is the center or core of all these things. All these come from the production room. In the natural, or flesh, realm, it is the most important part of your being. Proverbs 23:7 states: *"For as he (man) thinketh in his heart, so is he."* The thinking is done in a man's heart! The results of his thinking are what he becomes and does. It did not say, "as a man thinketh in his heart, so thinketh he." The Word of God says a man's thinking in his heart will produce or determine what he is and what he does. The word "thinketh" means to split or to open and act as a gatekeeper. In other words, as a man thinks, his heart acts as the gatekeeper to let things in or keep things out or keep things in and let things out.

It is important that we understand that the heart is not some passive part of us that utilizes osmosis to make things happen. No, it is very active, and an extremely important part of our being that determines our entire conduct and behavior. The heart acts as the **gatekeeper** of everything that is important and everything that determines how we conduct our lives. What an awesome position. Can you begin to see why many of the problems we have faced are because we did not know what the heart was or how it operated? But, if we get a revelation of the magnitude of just the "thinking" process in the heart, we will then make some new determinations about what we think.

Is Your Heart Sound?

Proverbs 14:30 tells us what the heart can produce: *"A sound heart is the life of the flesh."* The word sound, in this context, means: "curative, medicine, deliverance or remedy." Your sound heart can be the medicine and deliverance for your flesh. The condition of your heart determines what you will have in life. Will you succeed? Will you fail? Will you go on with God? Will you give up? Your heart will produce the outcome. Is your heart sound?

A sound heart is what made a disabled and disfigured Vietnam veteran named Dave Roever become a blessing to mankind, a minister of the Gospel, and a humorous uplifting individual. Blown apart by a grenade, he lost an ear (he now wears a removable one), lost fingers (and still plays the piano), had his eyes affected, and many other disabling things. Dave could have withdrawn into a shell of self-pity. He could have become a totally useless human being. He could be on welfare and have been taken care of by the government all of his life. Instead, he had a sound heart (remember the definition). The core, the center, the production room of his attitudes, of his senses, of his will, and of his emotions was sound. He said, "No. This will not cause me to be a nothing." He chose to fulfill God's plan for his life. That man has a sound heart, and that sound heart was medicine and deliverance to his flesh. Consequently, Dave Roever has ministered to and blessed thousands of people, and Father God is using him mightily for His glory.

Establishing the Boundaries of Your Heart

One of the key verses in our subject of study is Proverbs 4:23: *"Keep thy heart with all diligence; for out of it are the issues of life."* Let me give some definitions of this verse so we can dissect the meaning.

1. **Keep:** "to guard or protect."
2. **Diligence:** "a guard."

3. **Issues:** "exit, boundaries, a place from where things spring forth or go forth. It is also a source or border".

Keep thy heart—place a guard to protect the guard (double protection); an outer door to protect the inner part of your heart. Because out of the heart flow the issues—the boundaries, the borders, the springs of **LIFE**. This is the place where life springs forth or goes forth. I want to declare to you that everything we experience in life stems out of our heart. Our thoughts come out of our heart: "As *a man thinketh in his heart*...." Our heart is the producer and manufacturer of our emotions and attitudes. It is important to see that each area of our heart affects the other, and if one area is in a mess, all the other areas will also be—i.e., a line of thinking will produce more of the same and eventually affect the emotions and attitudes.

You might question why the devil is still attacking you when the Word of God says that we have victory over the devil. Since we have victory over the devil, why are we blaming him for all our problems and circumstances? We have been given power over him (Luke 10:19). We have authority to bind and loose on this earth (Matthew 16:19). God has given **us** the victory. Now we must **walk** in it. God has put you and me in a place of protection called "Abiding in Christ," or "walking in the spirit." But **we** open the door for the devil to enter. He loves to attack and affect your **thinking**. He knows how the heart works, and if he can get hold of your thinking, he does not have to do anything else— *"As a man thinketh, in his heart, so **IS** he..."* (Proverbs 23:7).

So the thoughts that take place in the heart determine the person, *"for out of the heart flow the issues (boundaries and borders) of **LIFE**"* (or death, depending on what you think). Proverbs 23:7 says, *"As a man thinketh in his heart, **SO IS HE**."* We have heard we are what we eat. This passage says what we think on in the heart will determine what we are and what we do. If the thoughts in my heart have no boundaries or borders set on them, then the things flowing out of my heart will not produce life but rather death. Remember, the Word of God must be the vehicle that produces the borders and boundaries in the heart. Are you beginning to see how important it is to think about the right things?

Paul, the Apostle wrote in Philippians 4:8: *"Whatever is true, honest, just, pure, lovely, of good report, things of virtue and praise…* **Think** *on these things."* So, the opposite is true also. If your thoughts do not fall into one of these areas, **DO NOT** think on them. How you may ask, do I not think on thoughts that I have? First, recognize that any thought contrary to the Word of God is from satan. Ephesians 6 speaks of fiery darts that are thrown at us by satan. But II Corinthians 10 tells us that we are to bring **every** thought into captivity to the obedience to Christ. So, if the thought is contrary to the Word of God, we are to verbally refuse the thought and command it to bow its knee to the Lordship of Christ. This is not easy, but it works. The thought will probably not go away the first time, but if you stay after it, I can tell you it will go away. But, for this to be effective, you must know the Word of God.

How then do we get into an arena where the devil can attack us with devastating thoughts? One major way is STRIFE! II Timothy 2:23-25 tells us that we open the door to the devil when we get into strife, arguing, or disagreements. The result (of being in strife) is stated in verse 26: *"We are taken captive by the devil, at **his** will."* Your will has nothing to do with it at that point. When you get in strife, it allows the devil to move in your life and have a party. So, it is vital to get the Word of God deeply planted in your heart so you can walk above any circumstance.

If you have ever been sick, you know that it is captivity. Even doctors, who know nothing about Jesus, will tell you about the effects of strife on a person's health. I had a psychiatrist friend tell me that every person he has ever counseled who had severe arthritis had a severe case of bitterness, unforgiveness, and resentment. We need to quit thinking and talking ugly about one another. That is strife! I have counseled people who had problems with their jobs or financial difficulties. One brother was having these difficulties. While we prayed, God revealed that the devil was holding him captive financially because of strife between him and his wife. We are the ones who hold the keys. Jesus got the keys back for us when He was raised from the dead. He came back holding the keys to death, hell, and the grave. Think about it—sickness, disease, financial misery, etc., is a step toward death. Jesus came to make us free. John 8:32 says, *"You shall know the truth, and the truth shall make you free."* Get the truth of this message of the heart inside you and watch freedom burst forth.

Attitude Makes All the Difference

I talk to a lot of people about various problems, and the one thing that is prevalent in all problems is bad attitudes. There is a lot of "stinking thinking" going on in the body of Christ that ought not to be. Do you know what determines our accomplishments in this life? It is not strictly our abilities. All of us have known people that had limited natural ability, yet they made significant contributions in life. On the other hand, we have known people that had all the ability in the world and accomplished zero or next to nothing in life. The difference is attitude. A person with resolve says that it doesn't make any difference what gets in their way; they are going to find a way to press through.

I am told that karate experts who break boards and bricks do not just look at the object in front of them. Rather, they look through or beyond the object and see themselves going through the object. Medical doctors have experienced this with their patients. Some patients with no medical hope or remedy get up and go home and get well. Other patients with no medically diagnosed physical problems enter the hospital, stay there, and die. The difference is that they just give up. Those that survive do so because their attitude gives them the drive to survive. A messed-up heart (wrong attitude) affects your entire life because it produces wrong thought patterns, which in turn produce wrong emotions. Soon thereafter, behavior consistent with those wrong thoughts but inconsistent with the Word of God takes you into a downward spiral that is hard to stop. I have good news!! Keep reading.

Have you ever battled wrong thoughts (immoral thoughts, for example)? You battle the thoughts and say, "Oh, God, I'm sorry, I'm sorry." You repent and truly are sorry but, five minutes later, or two minutes later, or ten seconds later, you are thinking the same thing. When your production room is turning out wrong thought patterns, you do not have a sound heart. You have a heart that does not have any boundaries on it, and those wrong thought patterns will cause you to go in the wrong direction. Mark 3:27 states: *"No man can enter into a strong man's house, and spoil his goods, except he will first bind the strong man; and then he will spoil his house."*

If we want to get wrong thought patterns, poor attitudes, and undisciplined emotions changed, we must attack the strong man. **The strong man is the heart.** The strong man is the center, the seat, and the authority of the production room of the mind, the will, the emotions, and the senses.

The Heart is Your Responsibility

I want you to know, the heart is not God's responsibility—it is our responsibility. My heart is **mine** to keep. Your heart is your responsibility. Proverbs 4:23 says: *"Keep thy heart with all diligence..."* The understood subject is **You**! You keep your heart with all diligence. God will not do it. You are to keep it. Will Father God help? A resounding YES; He has provided the tools with which we can keep it. For further confirmation, read the following verses:

- Proverbs 23:7: *"As a man thinketh in his heart...."*
- Proverbs 23:2: *"Apply thine heart to instruction."*
- Hebrews 3:8: *"Harden not your hearts."*

You are responsible for the thinking, applying, or hardening of your heart. Your heart is the seat (throne) of the whole issue of life. All authority resides in your heart for the control of the soulish realm. If we do not give diligent care to that part of our being, the soul will never come under control. Paul wrote in Romans 8:6, 7a: *"For to be carnally minded is death; but to be spiritually minded is life and peace. Because the carnal mind is enmity against God...."* To be carnally minded is to be controlled by the soul and not the spirit. The soul-controlled mind is an enemy of God. To walk in life and peace instead of in enmity against God, it is important to get the heart (remember the definition) under the control of the Word of God and out of the control of the flesh.

Chapter 2

The Fixed and Established Heart

To maintain our heart under the control of the Word of God, it needs to be **fixed** and **established**? Psalm 112:7-8 states: *"He shall not be afraid of evil tidings: his heart is fixed, trusting in the Lord. His heart is established, he shall not be afraid, until he sees his desire upon his enemies."* To put these verses in context, read all of Psalm 112. The "he" refers to the man or person that delights greatly in God's commandments (verse 1). What a tremendous attitude to have to delight greatly in God's commandments. When you get that attitude towards everything that God's Word says and respond, "Oh, I love to do that," you will be blessed. Psalm 112 continues promising the following specific blessings:

1. Your seed shall be mighty upon the earth.
2. Your generation shall be blessed.
3. Wealth and riches shall be in your house.
4. Your righteousness shall endure forever.
5. Light shall arise in the darkness.
6. You shall be gracious and full of compassion, and righteous.
7. You will have enough to lend to others.

8. You will guide your affairs with discretion.
9. You shall not be moved forever.
10. You shall be in everlasting remembrance.
11. And you shall not be afraid of evil tidings.

What tremendous promises and blessings are in store for those who greatly delight in God's Word and commandments. Blessings for your children; blessings upon your sowing; financial blessings; blessings of guidance; blessings of illumination and revelation; and blessings of freedom from fear. This Psalm clearly promises victory and freedom. I have determined to walk in the victory God has promised, and Jesus has won. These blessings result from delighting in God's Word, which causes the heart of man to become "**fixed**" and "**established**." A fixed and established heart results in victory, in blessings, and in freedom.

Does the Tail Wag the Dog?

Definition: a **fixed** heart is set or turned in a particular direction and given guidance. An **established** heart is one that is propped up or supported in some way as to maintain its direction or shape.

If my heart is not kept, or if it is left unguarded, and if it is not directed and given guidance, it will just go wild. So will yours. Our hearts need guarding! If you want to hear the good news, your heart will receive it—a heart always wants help and direction. But the heart is like a river. It will run all over the place if we don't have the banks built up properly—we have to prop it up. To prop up our heart, we must build some resistance within our heart so it cannot run any old direction it wants to. To do that takes hard work and consistency. My heart needs, wants and it must have those boundaries if it is going to be a heart like King David's. David was a man after God's own heart because he propped, fixed, and forced his heart to go in a particular direction—after God.

Once again it is our responsibility to prop up and force our heart to go in a particular direction. We must be daily conscientious about fixing our hearts and realize that we all have emotions that are good but must be guided and directed. When the emotions control the person, it is comparable to the tail wagging the dog. It should not be. Today, because of worldly influences, far too many Christians are being controlled by their emotions! None of us are immune from our emotions trying to rule in our lives. Take fear, for example, I know what fear will do to people, so I have said in my heart that I will not fear. I have set the direction for my heart and determined that I will not fear. I have established the banks: the boundaries within which my heart can flow freely. Now I must continue to prop up my heart so it will not run out of its banks and go in every direction.

One night I had finished studying and preparing my lesson for the church. At 11:00 p.m. I told my wife I was going out to walk around the neighborhood and pray. Now I have walked our neighborhood many times before, and it is a safe neighborhood. I had recently made the determination not to let my heart fear. As I walked around the neighborhood that night, I was confirming my commitment by saying, "I have no fear in my heart." Suddenly, there was a rustle in a bush because it was very windy. How I responded was amazing to me: goose bumps ran up and down my spine, and fear rose instantly in my heart. My temptation was to turn around immediately and head for the house. But then I said, "Wait a minute, my heart is fixed, and it will not fear!" I could feel my heart begin to settle down a little, so I proceeded further down the street. Then a piece of plastic struck a fence, and with the strong wind, it whistled and hummed, and I jumped a foot! There was the fear again! It was a phenomenal experience. I had directed my heart, yet every little thing that moved caused fear to rise. Had I not kept after my heart, I would have been a nervous wreck by the time I got back to the house. But I continued to say, "NO! My heart is fixed, it will not fear, my heart is not full of fear, it is full of peace." I want you to know that we all have an opportunity to fear.

There will always be challenges to the direction you have set to fix your heart. The ways of the flesh, directions, and training of the world in which we used to live are in direct opposition to God's thoughts and ways. Consequently, our hearts may fight and rebel at the new direction and guidance we give it. The good news is that the heart can be fixed and established. But we must keep at it and be relentless. We cannot just "let it go" because it will not just "fall into place." The heart has been untrained for too long, and we must take the offensive even if we must **"be"** offensive. The fixing and establishing of your heart is absolutely vital to spiritual health and direction. If we ever hope to be led by the Spirit, we must have a heart that has boundaries and focus. If we ever hope to fulfill our destiny, we must give the heart guidance and determination and allow the Spirit of God to lead and guide us into all truth. A heart that has been allowed to go and do whatever it desires cannot receive revelation knowledge, let alone act on anything that we might have come to understand.

My Garden Analogy

The need to fix and establish our hearts reminds me of my summer endeavors at gardening. I really enjoy growing a garden. Every spring I dig each row and get all the rows seeded or planted just right. I then place a furrow between rows to water what I had planted. After digging the furrow beside each row, I irrigate with my garden hose. As the water travels down the furrow and makes its way down the row, you must prop up and build up the banks, so the path becomes established. You must keep a close eye on the irrigation as it is easy for the water, after coursing down the furrow, to find a weak spot and go out of bounds. Once that water has found a weak spot, it will always find another. So, you must watch it constantly. When the water gets out of its boundaries (the furrow) it runs over the entire garden and maybe even into your neighbor's yard causing a real mess. This is exactly what the heart does. If you do not prop up, guide, and direct the flow of your heart, it will cause a mess for you and many others around you.

To remedy this situation in the garden, you get down in the mud and prop up, build up, and plug up the weak spot or hole. You must build up the banks so that water goes down the fixed row where you want it to go. When you do this, you have established the furrow as being the direction **you** want the water to travel. The water wants to go many other directions, and left alone, and it will go everyplace you do not want it to go. Likewise, the heart, it will go wherever it wants to go based on past training.

Our hearts are just like the water. A battle is waged in the heart over the course or direction to be traveled. God wants us to go in His direction. Emotions, flesh, or our own will pull us in the opposite direction. Any time your thoughts, emotions, senses, or actions go a different direction from what you have fixed your heart to do, your heart is out of its banks. It is running all over the place, and you must prop and build up the banks by speaking the Word of God and reminding your heart of the proper course or direction to take. It will take some work, but the results will be very rewarding. **CAUTION**: Do not try to make boundaries for your heart without the Word of God as the source.

Anger, bitterness, resentment, and unforgiveness are holes in the furrow of the heart that is fixed towards walking in love. But Father God wants us to take His Word and deal with them. There is no place in a Christian's life for these emotions. God has told us not to let them rule our hearts. Many people do not know what to do to correct their emotions, and they lose in a wrestling match with them. It's only with the Word of God that we can win the struggle. We may experience a lot of garbage in relationships or circumstances, but we are determined not to allow it to do anything to us. We determine our hearts are fixed and established and full of peace, love, and joy.

I have battled my share of discouragement as a pastor. But I want you to know that I have determined that my heart is fixed and established. I am going to do what God has told me to do! That does not mean that once you say, "Alright, heart, you are fixed," it is fixed forever. Once you have fixed your heart and established it and propped it up, you will have plenty of opportunities for it to change course or run over its banks. You must stick to the decision and direction you have determined for your heart. Rest assured; any direction contrary to the way your heart has always gone will face opposition. Your heart is a creature of habit, and it does not necessarily like change. But thank God for His Word that is stronger than your heart.

If you are battling emotional hurts, unforgiveness, bitterness, and anger, I want you to know your props have fallen, your channel is leaking, and your heart is not directed. If your thoughts are running wild, you are considering how to get even and meditating on revenge, or you are struggling before God with the thought of why you are in your present emotional state, enough is enough! Glory to God, you will soon understand that you can control your mind and heart!

Your Control Over Willpower and Emotion

To prove that you can control your mind, I want you to imagine for a minute that you are at the zoo. Now, in your imagination, see yourself go into the monkey house and look at the Orangutan. He has shaggy, reddish-brown hair with very long arms. He is about four feet tall, and his face is hairless and ugly. The most obvious is his orange bottom. Do you see him? Now, you are **not** at the zoo, so stop thinking about that Orangutan. But, once you have spent time meditating on the image of the Orangutan, it is hard to stop thinking about the ape. It would be tougher if I would have talked about food, especially if you are hungry. But see, whenever you set your mind in a channel, your mind will follow the set direction.

One of the biggest lies from Satan is that you cannot control your emotions, your willpower, or your thoughts in your heart. For instance, consider a smoking habit. Some of you have wrestled with that habit and may still be wrestling with it. I want you to know that the biggest lie is that **YOU CANNOT STOP!** You may not know what to do to stop, but you <u>can</u> stop. What happens is this: you make the decision to stop smoking, and you set the boundaries of your heart and give it some guidelines. Now, your heart is going the "I will not smoke direction," and for whatever reason, you get to a hole in the furrow of your heart that says **SMOKE**, and your heart runs out of its banks. Then the heart tells you it is no use to try to quit, so you might as well go ahead and smoke. But that is not the right answer. You just need to plug the hole where your heart is getting out of bounds. You can stop anything when you get your heart (the production room of those thoughts) going the way of God.

I see some of you reading this book and saying, "OH THANK GOD," because you feel that your hope is being restored. That's wonderful because there is so much hope for each one of you. The problem is in your heart. Understand that it has not been forced to go in a certain direction before and has been allowed to run wild. You have not demanded it stay in the channel where the Word of God describes that it should be. The problem is that you do not know what you do not know because you do not know what you do not know. Selah!

Anytime we fix and establish our heart to go in a particular direction, it is then that we discover the holes in the banks, and our heart begins to run out of bounds. As I stated before, the major thing we face is the lie that says, "You failed, and you will NEVER overcome that area of WEAKNESS." But that's not the truth. JUST GO PLUG THE HOLE and move forward in your set direction again with determination and the Word of God. When I am in my garden and place the hose in the furrow and direct the water down the row, should I look down and see the water running out of the furrow, I will not just stand there and say, "It won't go down the row." No, I go down and prop up the hole and build up the bank so the water will go where I want it to go. It will not do so on its own, so I guide and direct it.

What about our problems with our hearts? We have had some attitude problems, some thinking problems, but we have failed to recognize that we are the ones that direct our heart to go where it should go. Our heart always wants to run out of bounds until it is **well** established. Like the water in the garden furrow, after I have run water down my garden row a dozen times or so, I no longer have to supervise the watering. I just place the hose in the row, and it goes the proper way as the channel is fixed and established. That is our goal: **A Fixed and Established heart.**

Many folks have not formed the banks of their heart. They do not have a well-defined, directed, and established furrow for their heart. Instead of a furrow-irrigated heart, their heart is more like a sprinkler that sprays water every way and on everything in the way. Have you ever tried to walk by one of those jitterbug sprinklers? It seems that no matter which way you go, you will still get splattered. The thoughts and emotions of this "sprinkler" heart have been spraying all over the place. You cannot get around or be around this "sprinkler" heart without getting wet and splattered. It is just a mess and not fun to be around. Our heart needs to be fixed and established like a furrow in a garden and watered by a single stream of the garden hose of God's Word.

Our misunderstanding of the heart has misled us in trying to fix the problems we have faced. When we should have been taking the Word of God and getting our hearts **fixed and established**, we have done so many other things that have not worked. Consequently, many have lost hope and have given up. Typically, when we encounter the problems that we face, our common approach has been to rebuke the devil and cast this demon and that demon out. I am not saying that the devil should not be cast out. I am saying that it is the wrong approach in fixing and establishing the heart. The correct key is found in II Corinthians 10:4-5: *"The weapons of our warfare are not carnal, but mighty through God to the pulling down of strongholds, casting down imaginations and every high thing that exalteth itself against the knowledge of God, and bringing into captivity every thought to the obedience of Christ...."*

Weapons are for warfare. Our spiritual weapons are not carnal or thought up by you or some psychologist. The last passage of scripture clearly points out we are to **work** at pulling down the strongholds—more descriptively called "strangleholds." These are situations that strangle the very life out of you. Strongholds are those things that plague you and bug you and never seem to go away. They are issues and habits that you just cannot seem to break or get over. As we continue in this passage in verse 5, let us notice a connection between these strongholds and thoughts—we are to bring into captivity **every** thought!

Let me take a side trail for a moment to explain a progression that takes place that will help you understand this passage. Notice when you reverse the order of this passage how it begins with thoughts. Thoughts (which happen to be the fiery darts of Satan in Ephesians 6) produce an image. Should I say to you, "dog," you would have an image of a dog? Now, if I said, "big black dog," your image probably changed. So, thoughts that are contrary to the Word of God and not dealt with (brought into captivity to the obedience of Christ) will produce an imagination that exalts itself against the knowledge of God. That imagination allowed to go unchecked will then gain a stronghold in your heart first, then in your life. So how do we get control?

As we have discussed, the very center or origination point of your thoughts is in the heart. But do you know it is impossible for strongholds to be pulled down, imaginations cast down, and thoughts brought into the obedience of Christ without God on the **throne** of your heart? It simply will not be done. You cannot bring those thoughts into captivity with your own might, regardless of how hard you try. Are you having difficulty breaking habits that disturb you and harass you? Have you tried and tried to get free from some irritating issue even with prayer and maybe fasting, but to no avail? Unless Father God is on the throne of your heart, you will continue to fail. But I have good news! The weapons of our warfare are not carnal; they are not of the flesh but are mighty through God—and the strongholds can come down. It is important to realize that strongholds and imaginations are in your heart. Your heart is where indifference, rebellion, and lethargy are located. But we have mighty non-carnal weapons that are a gift from God.

Your heart is either the greatest force in your life today, or it may be your greatest problem. Let me make a radical statement: God is not the greatest force in your life until He gains ascendancy in your heart. God will not violate your "will," which comes out of the origination point of your heart. The question we must ask is: "How in the world do I get my heart fixed and established so I can be successful in my life? Then, how do I begin to get God on the throne of my heart? What am I supposed to look for?"

Keep reading, and I will teach you how to get God on the throne of your heart.

Chapter 3

How to Have a "Want to" Heart

Most Christians have not been taught what makes up the heart. In fact, most believe it is only the organ that pumps the blood. Physically yes, that is its function, but I have good news for you; the heart I'm talking about is different. It is the spiritual heart. God says, *"You will know the truth, and the truth will make you free"* (John 8:32). We need to walk in that truth, freedom, and victory to such a degree that nothing or no one can take it away from us. But the sorry situation is that too many Christians are in bondage, fighting multiple battles with all sorts of worries and problems.

In your wildest imagination, can you see a picture of God all bound up with problems? No! Well, the Word of God says that we are made in His image and likeness. Should we be bound up with problems? No! That is why God spoke through the Apostle John: *"As He (Jesus) is, so are we in this world..."* (I John 4:17). He could only say something like that because God knows how well He has created and equipped us. He is familiar with the tools and weapons He has given us. Because He made us in His own image and likeness, we should not be bound up with problems.

To walk in the freedom, we must learn how to use the Word of God as a weapon and apply the truth of the Word of God to develop the heart. Then we will be empowered to perform just like Jesus. God says, *"My people are destroyed for a lack of knowledge..."* (Hosea 4:6). If we have not availed ourselves of the Word of God and learned the truths to operate in the power of a fixed and established heart, we will never see ourselves operate like Jesus. If you say: "Man, I have never acted like Jesus." Keep on reading—I am going to teach you how to do just that!

Have you ever known somebody who was bound up in drugs, alcohol, or other negative habits or problems and liked it? Most people do not like to have ongoing struggles and be driven by habits that plague them. It's like that for people in prison—whether guilty or not guilty—they don't like being in prison. Nobody likes being in the pits. All men everywhere are longing for two things: peace and joy! And they'll try anything to get it. Unfortunately, the world's remedies are temporary, and they don't last. When people come down from a drug-high or alcohol binge, immediately they're faced with the same problems, and they find they are back in the pits. The cry of mankind is to be free, and the key to that freedom is "Keeping the heart."

The Issues of Life

I mentioned in a previous chapter that a sound heart is life to the flesh (Proverbs 14:30). The word "sound" in this passage in the Hebrew text means "curative, medicine, deliverance or remedy." I am not talking about the blood pump. If a sound heart is life to the flesh, it tells me if I have been sick a lot that I should be checking out the condition of my heart. Sickness is never life; it is the manifestation of death—with some sicknesses being greater degrees of death than other illnesses! We know when an x-ray is taken, the diseased part shows up cloudy and abnormal. Such is a heart that is allowing sickness: cloudy and abnormal.

The Bible shows us that all things originate from the heart when it states: *"Keep thy heart with all diligence, for out of **IT** are the issues of life"* (Proverbs 4:23). **"IT"** refers to the heart. Out of the heart proceed all the issues of life. Everything we face in life has to do with the heart. Now, you may not like that comment or what I am showing you, but you need to see it even if the truth hurts. I want to help you overcome the struggles and problems that are continually plaguing you. Matthew 12:35 states: *"A good man out of the good treasure of his heart bringeth forth good things: and an evil man out of the evil treasure bringeth forth evil things."* A good man cannot have a bad heart. It is impossible! Similarly, an evil man cannot have a good heart. Your heart cannot be aimed in many different directions. It is either set toward good or evil. Evil means hurtful or calamitous. Out of an evil heart will come hurtful or calamitous words or deeds. Conversely then, a good heart will bring forth good words and good things.

Wishy-Washy and Double-Minded

James 1:8 says it so perfectly: *"A double-minded man is unstable in **all** of his ways."* It doesn't say most of his ways. It says **ALL OF HIS WAYS**! That does not leave anything out. According to James, a double-minded man is going one way and fifteen minutes later is seen going in the opposite direction. If someone teaches you something one day, causing you to change direction in your life, but the next day you go another way—you are wishy-washy. It means you have taken a stand for God now, but later, "Well, I better do this instead." If you desire your issues of life to go God's way, then you are going to have to take a stand for God. God commissions the angels to the task of ministering for you (Hebrews 1:14). If you could only see into the realm of the spirit, you would see that just about the time the angels are departing to minister to you in a situation, you change your words, and then your mind and God must put a hold on the angels' orders until you decide what you really want. That is instability, wish-washy, indecision, wavering, or double-mindedness.

The KEY to this fitting together with the heart is in James 4:8: *"Purify your hearts, ye double-minded."* The problem of double mindedness is not in the spirit realm. IT IS IN THE heart! God is saying if you purify your heart, you will not be double-minded. The Bible says that *"out of the heart are the issues of life"* (Proverbs 4:23), and Matthew 12:35 says evil things in your life come from an evil heart. This tells me we cannot place blame on God, on our wife, on our husband, or on our parents for our problems. Rather than blame anybody, let's face the fact that the problems come from an evil heart. Look at yourself in the mirror of God's Word and face up to it. That is why evil things are coming out of you and out of me. That is why hurtful calamitous things are happening. We must understand that even though it is easier to blame everybody else, freedom will only come when we look in the mirror and say, "the problem is me."

Do you remember the Bible account of King David when the prophet Nathan exposed David's sin of adultery with Bathsheba and murder of Uriah (II Samuel 11 and 12)? David's first response was: *"The man that committed that crime should be put to death"* (12:5). Nathan replied: *"That man is you"* (12:7). Do you know why David was called a man after God's own heart? As a King, he could have had the prophet killed and silenced. But how could he rid his heart of the thought: "You are the man?" David proved to be a man after God's own heart because he quickly repented and honestly dealt with evil in his heart.

We need to realize Christians can have evil, hurtful, calamitous hearts. So how do we get our hearts right? First, we must understand that the heart is not the spirit. The heart is the seat (core, center) of the intellect, the emotions, the senses, the desire, the appetites, and the will. It is a part of the soul, <u>but not the totality of the soul</u>. Your soul is the **storage** room, but the heart is the **production** room. It is the manufacturing room where all the senses, desires, appetites, passions, will, and intellect spring forth from mankind. That is why the Bible states in Matthew 12:35: *"out of the evil treasure of the heart, evil things* *come forth, and out of the good treasure of the heart good things come forth."*

A lot of Christians have difficulty keeping their bodies under control. I am a Pastor. I counsel, I get the phone calls. From experience, I know about the struggles people are having. The problem is that the production room is faulty and double-minded. Consider the following examples: you speak well of a person one day and knife them in the back with critical words the next; you are on fire for God one day, blessing the body of Christ, and then you disappear and don't come to church for months. I think you know what I'm talking about. Keeping the body under control is a major problem in the church today.

Wrong Thoughts—Wrong Actions!

What causes double mindedness? Wrong thoughts! I never struggled against getting drunk or smoking marijuana or cigarettes. Those activities have never been problems for me because I never think about them. In fact, I would rather get high on the Holy Spirit. I know to think on carnal things is DEATH: death to your body, morally and spiritually! When you think about carnal things, they get into the production room, and as you dwell on that garbage, you will produce in those areas. *"As a man thinketh in his heart, so IS he"* (Proverbs 23:7). Do we think in our minds? Of course, but the production room of the mind is in your heart. As a man thinketh in his heart, **SO IS HE**. The reason people become alcoholics is due to WRONG thoughts. People will experience some measure of success from time to time and may stay sober for a while, but all the evil thoughts, if not reversed, will affect them, and they will begin feeling sorry for themselves or get angry about something, and their thinking and their emotions go down into the pits. Their wrong thoughts lead them right back to the pit, and from there, it is a close step back to the bottle.

To gain control of your body and keep it under control, you must control your mind. If you do not have control of your mind, you are going to become or do something you may not want to be or do. This struggle is going on in people everywhere. Paul talked about this in the book of Romans: "I don't want to do that" and yet "I end up doing it" (Romans 7; Author Paraphrase). I believe that the basic cause of this persistent problem is caused by not controlling your mind and the wrong thoughts that enter it. How wonderful it would be to be able to flip a switch and change your thought patterns. At times, we all would like to be able to do that. Unfortunately, it's very difficult, if not impossible, to do because an evil man, out of the evil treasure of his heart, brings forth evil things. So, if the Word of God is true and it is our basis of truth, then the problem is in the heart: the manufacturing and producing station for all of the desires, the appetites, and the thought patterns in our life.

Don't Be A "Fruit Picker!"

As a believer, you should not pick the fruit of your evil heart and hope that nobody notices. But, if you are truthful, that is what you have done—pick the fruit off and hope no one sees that you drink, smoke, cuss, chew, watch pornography, have road rage, or abuse your spouse. Be assured, picking the fruit of an evil heart may only cover up the problem temporarily to those who are around you, but you know the truth, and so does your Father God. Whatever you do, do not prune those evil things because when you prune a tree, it will grow and produce more. To deal with evil fruit, you must go for the root of the problem: the heart. The fruit is only an outward expression of what the root is producing. **GO FOR THE ROOT!**

In the last chapter, we discussed getting your heart fixed. I described how I established the furrows in my garden so the water would travel down the rows. During the times, however, when the water tried to overrun the banks, I had to fix the banks to ensure the water would go where I wanted it to go. So, it is with our heart. We must fix our heart by plugging the holes using the Word of God, and then our thinking will be straightened out—a process that also straightens out our **WILL**. When your will and desires are in line with God's Word, the outflow of that will be right living. When you find you are having a heart struggle like the Apostle Paul: the things you do not want to do, you do; and the things you want to do, you do not do; thank God there is no condemnation.

It is important to realize that the responsibility of keeping and fixing the heart is **YOURS**! God will help you every step of the way, but you must take responsibility. It is more than asking God to change your heart, or even singing that song: "Change my heart Oh, God," because usually, the next phrase which comes out your mouth is: "Oh, man, I feel so bad today; Oh, the finances are terrible; Oh, I will probably get laid off my job." Listen, you are not helping God with that kind of mouth. For every problem we have, we rely upon Him and that includes a messed up heart—because God promised He would give us a new one.

Psalms 33:13-15 states: *"The Lord looketh from heaven; He beholdeth all the sons of men. From the place of his habitation He looketh upon all the inhabitants of the earth. He fashioneth their hearts alike; He considereth all their works."* Look at how Psalms 33 states: *"all the sons of men"*. That phrase leaves nobody out. The word "fashioneth" in this passage means that God squeezed it into an identical shape. ALL the inhabitants of the earth, all men's hearts were fashioned to do His will. I want to tell you that is shouting news. God has not destined one man to do evil things, and another to do good things, and yet another to do mediocre things, and someone else to be a bum. He has made all hearts alike. Please know that ALL ALIKE is the VICTORIOUS ALIKE!

When we see men involved in sin, we know for sure that God has not made them for that kind of life. God did not fashion their hearts for them to ignore Him committing adultery, murder, and all manner of sin. God is the one that fashioned men's hearts, and He has given the same desires, the same appetites, and the same passions to every man. If any of those desires and passions and appetites is contrary to God, you can be confident that God did not create them that way—somewhere along the way, the heart has gotten messed up, wrecked, and perverted. God created our hearts to walk in the perfection of His will, not sometimes making it and sometimes missing it. The bottom line is: He has fashioned our hearts and placed in us, and given to us the "**WANT TO**" so that we can accomplish the perfection of His will.

Now, if you say, "I just do not seem to have the 'want to,'" well, it's just been lost somewhere because on the day of your conception, God gave it to you. God designed your heart so you could walk with as much ease in serving Him as is possible for flesh and blood people who live in a world of sin. We should not be fighting the hellish war tormenting us inside our hearts. Double-minded man, you go this way one day and over there, another. Pulled by sin one way and pulled by the Holy Spirit the other way. It is a back and forth, up and down, battle. God did <u>not</u> create us to be in that kind of struggle. Conflict of any kind can be <u>around</u> you, and it can be coming from the outside towards you but, the inner conflict should not exist. God did not form us to have the "want to" toward sin or the carnal desires of the flesh. He called us to peace.

There are lots of people who have the "want to" to sin. But God formed our hearts so that we would have the "want to" towards HIM. God wants us walking in His ways, wanting to do His ways, thrilled, and delighted with doing His ways. Are you really delighted to go God's way? Or is it something you do because you know you are required to. Are you excited about reading your Bible? Are you excited about spending time in prayer? Are you looking forward to going to church? That is how God created us. He not only loves you, He likes you. Isaiah 49:16 states that He (Father God) has graven or carved us on the palms of His hands. You are that special to Him. Just know that you can have a "want to" heart.

A New Heart and a New Spirit

Ezekiel 36:26 says: *"A new heart also will I give you and a new spirit will I put within you: and I will take away the stony heart out of your flesh, and I will give you an heart of flesh."* This scripture states that the heart and the spirit are two different things. What is meant by a stony heart versus a heart of flesh? God is saying: "I am going to put within you a new heart that is going to have the "want to" for following Me." The word heart in this verse is the same Hebrew word all three times. But the phrase "Heart of flesh" refers to one (Heart) that can be touched or has freshness and that is full. God is going to put a heart into us that is easily touched. Not with human hands, but a heart that God can touch. God touched David's sensitive heart, making David quick to repent.

The phrase "I will put a new heart in you" refers to God giving you a new willingness. Now we do not have to be very smart in theology to figure out that there is a flaw in all of this: you! God will never violate the will He created you with, nor will He ever force you to do anything. Since you have a will and God chooses not to violate that will, how does all of this fit together? A new heart from God will give you a changed will! How do I get a new heart from God and a new will from God without Him violating my will? It happened at salvation when you received a new heart.

> Ephesians 3:14-17 states: *"For this cause, I bow my knees unto the Father of our Lord Jesus Christ of whom the whole family in heaven and earth is named, that He would grant you according to the riches of His glory, to be strengthened with might by His spirit in the inner man; that Christ may dwell in your* hearts, *by faith."*

Christ will dwell in our hearts by faith. He will take up residence in, abide in and settle down in our hearts. By faith, Christ is seated on the throne of your heart at salvation. At that point, Christ is on the throne, the production room of your thoughts, attitudes, and appetites. The Word of God says that He will dwell there by faith. Whose faith? HIS FAITH. You and I cannot produce an ounce of faith. We even got saved on the faith of God. Ephesians 2:8 says: *"For by grace are you saved, through faith, and that, not of yourselves, it is a gift of God."*

Picture a lost man (a sinner man) who has been living his life for the devil. He has previously had no desire for God, and he cannot produce an ounce of faith. Thank God, He gives us the faith wherewith we can be saved. Remember Romans 12:3 says: *"God has given to every man the measure of faith."* Faith is first for all to get saved. On his own, the lost man cannot produce an ounce of faith—God has placed the faith **in** him. This fellow has had no desire for God and has really walked in the opposite direction from God. He has not thought about God, except maybe to use His name as a swear word. Let me remind you that his heart was fashioned by God for the things of God. Even though this fellow cannot produce an ounce of faith, at one point, he responds to the gospel message and says: "I make Jesus the Lord of my life." What he did was set aside human reasoning, and by faith, accepted Jesus as his Lord. Immediately, a miracle happened: Jesus steps onto the throne of that sinner's heart. Because the sinner, by an act of his will, said, "You may have it." Do you see how God can give him a new heart? By believing, he activated the God-given faith when he accepted Jesus as Lord, giving his consent (his will) that Christ could dwell in his heart.

God gives us the seed of faith to be able to accept Him and gives His Word that will further activate that seed (Romans 10:17) that He planted in us. In doing so, He avoids violating our will since we WILL ourselves to accept Jesus. At that point, Christ immediately takes up residence on the throne of our heart and dwells there. The resulting change within the sinner is a new set of desires, attitudes, thoughts, and a new will. It is by a willful act that Christ comes into the heart, and the heart is changed! This changed person "wants to" come to church, "wants to" read the Bible, and "wants to" be just like Jesus. Yes, a changed heart can make you a fanatic because zeal and fire are kindled. Now it's very important to be discipled in the Word of God so old habits can be broken. Unfortunately, the long-time saved Christian says: "He will settle down after a while and become like us." But II Corinthians 5:17 states: *"If any man be in Christ, he is a new creature (creation), old things (a contrary heart) are **passed away**, behold (look and see) **ALL** things have become new."*

What about the rest of us who are fighting that war within, wanting the world and wanting God? If I am fighting, are you telling me that I do not have Jesus on the throne of my heart? I am not trying to tell you anything. You tell me whether He is on the throne of your heart or not. Examine the desires, thoughts, and appetites that you have. Scrutinize the words that come out of your mouth: *"Out of the abundance of the heart, the mouth talks"* (Matthew 12:34; Author Paraphrase).

I sadly report that many Christians today do not have Christ on the throne of their heart. They are cool or lukewarm. It is difficult to get them to do anything for God. They barely make it to church once a week, and they are half in the church, half in the world, and are double-minded. James states it clearly: *"Purify your heart, you double-minded...."* (James 4:8). It is a heart problem. How do I get Jesus back on the throne of my heart? He was there once, and He may still be there in some areas of your heart. Please continue reading. I do not intend to leave you hanging in the wind by stating the problems without offering solutions. God reveals the problem so we can correct it and be lifted out of the mess.

Chapter 4

How to Get Christ Back on the Throne of Your Heart

We have begun to delve into the Word of God in an area that is so deep and rich. I encourage you to read the scriptures over and over, meditate on what God has said, pray in the spirit, and ask the Holy Spirit to illuminate the meaning of the Word we have discussed. This word must become revelation knowledge in your heart because it is difficult to act on anything that does not become a revelation to you!

Prior to this chapter, we described the heart and its importance in the believer's life. Recall, the heart is the very seat, center, and core of your senses, your emotions, your will, your intellect, your desires, your appetites, and your passions. Also remember, that at salvation, by an act of your will, Christ entered your heart and took His proper place on the throne of your heart by faith. That is the way God fashioned every man's heart for Christ to rule and reign there. But we have a sovereign "will," and our "will" can be opposed to God's "will."

At salvation, God changed our will and gave us the "want to" to love and serve Him. If that is so, how do we account for the turmoil, struggle, confusion, and the striving taking place within our hearts? If Jesus changed our will, our desires, and our appetites, how do we explain the unrest that occurs within us? The Holy Spirit desires His way in our hearts and lives. God does not want us spiritually on fire today and an ice cube tomorrow. The Christian life does not have to be a peak experience today and a low valley tomorrow. The biggest obstacle that is getting in our way is called pride, "the self." It is <u>soul control,</u> not <u>spirit control</u>.

The Self Test

A good test to determine your level of "self" comes during a time in a church service. Do you enter the service like the Bible teaches? Do you praise with joy like King David, perhaps with shouting, dancing, clapping, and singing? King David rejoiced before God. Do you need to check your attitude? You may lack knowledge, not understanding that God commands you to praise Him. But what is your reaction? Pride says: "What would others think or say about me." Pride also says, "We do not do that at our church, or I was not raised that way." Make the decision; Christ is going to be on the throne of my heart. David, who was not a born-again man (lived under the old covenant), danced with all his might and was completely sold out to God. We can do it under the new covenant with God's grace. I have made that decision, and if you have not, I encourage you to do so. We do not need to conform to this world, or to religion, or man's doctrine that is contrary to the doctrine of Christ.

Pride is a demon and a thief. The Bible states: *"God resisteth the proud, but giveth grace unto the humble..."* (James 4:6). In Proverbs 16:18, God says: *"Pride goeth before destruction, and an haughty spirit before a fall."* I do not want you to fall. I want all of you coming into the fullness of God. God wants you free from all heart turmoil and warfare more than I. Do not offer excuses or blame others, please. We must look in the mirror, and pride must go! Break up your fallow ground. The "Word of God" must be sown in a good heart.

Jesus said: *"No man putteth new wine into old bottles; else the new wine will burst the bottles and be spilled..."* (Mark 2:21). Old bottles break, and old wineskins get dry and brittle. An old wineskin must be reworked by rubbing oil on it. When it becomes pliable, you refill it. This is what we need. The anointing oil of the Holy Spirit must be applied, massaged, and worked into our hearts. When our hearts are soft, the Word of God can penetrate and be fruitful. On the contrary, a hard heart will not allow the Word of God to penetrate it.

Have you been listening to the Word being preached on television, radio, or CD's, yet wondering why nothing or very little is happening for you? Ask the Holy Spirit: "Do I have a hard heart?" As the anointing oil of the Holy Spirit massages and softens our hearts, we can receive the Word of God and begin to experience the relationship with God we desire. We will begin to flow in the anointing of the Holy Spirit, which will set us free to experience the freshness, vitality, and excitement we had when we were born again. It will be back.

Think about when you were first born again. Your excitement could not be contained. You spouted off to everyone. You had to tell somebody about God's goodness. It was more dramatic, for some, but you knew the life and love of God. But, because we have not known to keep our heart, we have lost it. If we allow the Word of God and the anointing oil of the Holy Spirit in our hearts, we can kick out the pride. Look at yourself in the mirror and make the determination to rid your heart of all pride. If you are serious, ask God to break you. A breaking experience will get rid of pride. Pride and ego are nothing more than counterfeits for Faith. It is the soul—that part of man that was never intended to make independent decisions apart from God—that still wants to be in control. Your spirit is to be in control, working under the authority of the Holy Spirit and working in conjunction with the heart that is fashioned by God.

What is Your Desire Upon the Enemy?

Psalms 112:1 says, *Praise ye the Lord. Blessed is the man that feareth the Lord, that delighteth greatly in his commandments."* In that passage, I believe that God is talking about a man with a "want to" heart. The only way you can have the "want to" is with Christ on the throne of your heart. Then you will delight greatly in His commandments. You will "want to" do all of God's Word. If God says, "Shout," you will shout. If God says: "Run around the building," you run around the building. If you see instruction in the Word of God, determine to do it, regardless of feelings or circumstances. There are a lot of hearers, but the doer is the one that is blessed.

The second verse of Psalms 112 is: *"His seed shall be mighty upon the earth."* Parents, do you want your children to be mighty upon the earth? Get Christ on the throne of your heart (with the

"Want to" to love and serve God) and let your children see that. Bless God and transmit good things to your children. Pass on to them the knowledge that "Christ is on the throne of your heart and He fills your every thought." *"Train up a child in the way he should go, and when he is old, he will not depart from it"* (Proverbs 22:6) does not say that they will depart after the training and later return. It says that they will not depart at all!

The next verse (3) of Psalms 112 states: *"Wealth and riches shall be in his house and his righteousness endureth forever."* Wow! Now we're getting into a prosperity message. When Christ is on the throne of your heart, wealth and riches shall be in your house. If you are experiencing lack, perhaps you need to examine your heart. It's not always an easy lesson, but it can be very profitable in your walk with God.   Part of that verse also says, *"his righteousness endureth forever."* With Christ on the throne of your heart, you will not live a roller coaster life—up one day and down the next: on fire for God one day and in sin the next. An enthroned Christ will cause your right standing with God to be a forever thing instead of a passing thing. It will be a habitation of Christ and not a visitation.

Part of verse 4 says: *"Unto the upright there ariseth a light in the darkness."* With Christ on the throne, light can enter your upright heart. Psalms112:8 states: *"His heart is established; he shall not be afraid until he sees his desire upon his enemies."* A fixed and established heart will see his desire upon his enemy. Your enemy is the devil. What is your desire towards the devil? My desire is to be so developed in the things of God that the devil knows my name and knows better than to get too close to me. My desire, when I awake in the morning, is to have the devil declare, **"Oh no, he's up."** My desire is to be walking and enforcing the victory that Jesus provided and walking with such authority that the words of Jesus will be totally true in my life.

When Jesus said: *"Nothing shall by any means hurt you"* (Luke 10:19), it was based on having an established and fixed heart. We, in the body of Christ, have become so devil-conscious it is pathetic. If your heart is right before God with Christ on the throne, the devil cannot touch you (I John 5:18). He is defeated (Hebrews 2). Otherwise, why would he have to use deception? Do not mistake this as condemnation. It is the truth. If the devil has been stomping on you, just grit your teeth, and fix and establish your heart. When your heart is right with God, you will only walk in goodness. Psalms 23:6 states, *"Surely, goodness and mercy will follow me all the days of my life."* You will not walk in evil but good. You will not be consumed with thoughts about the devil but rather about the Lord Jesus Christ, who loves you and gave Himself for you and defeated the devil.

Remember, Jesus said, *"out of my heart I will bring forth good treasure and good things because there is a good treasure in my heart"* (Matthew 12:35). I will only walk in good things when my heart is right. *"For this is the covenant that I will make with the house of Israel after those days, saith the Lord; I will put my laws into their minds, and write them in their hearts: and I will be to them a God, and they shall be to me a people"* (Hebrews 8:10). The church is the spiritual house of Israel. We who have believed are the ones God is talking about in this passage. God has put His laws in our heart and given us the "want to" to follow Him. At the time of the new birth (salvation), God gave us a new heart that changed our whole set of values. As I said earlier, salvation is very dramatic for some folks. No matter how dramatic our conversion, we all have found our desires, appetites, and passions were changed. That was the new heart that God promised you.

After we were born again, the responsibility for tending the heart was ours. It is absolutely the most important thing that we must do. WE cannot be passive about it. Until knowledge comes, we are totally passive, primarily because we have not known what to do. But, once my garden is planted, and furrows dug beside the rows of seeds, I cannot lay out on my lounge chair and relax. I must supervise the irrigation; I have to pull weeds, thin plants and tend to all the garden chores. My wife enjoys the fruit of my labor, but the garden work and responsibility are mine. In like manner, do not expect your wife, husband, pastor, neighbor, or God to tend your heart—it is your job. To repeat and emphasize, you simply cannot be passive when it comes to your heart.

Worldly Influence

How many of you know our society is in a mess and directly affects us (Christians)? Consider the television programs written and produced by unregenerate men and transmitted into our homes, telling us (Christians) how to think and act. They have influenced entirely too much of our thinking! Turn on the tube, and you see adultery, fornication, divorce, homosexuality, murder, rape, and all kinds of violence. Yet so many of us keep watching that junk! We let the sinners decide our clothing and dress fashions, even our mannerisms. As we watch that stuff, it gets into our hearts. Soon, we do not even think anything about it as it becomes commonplace.

For instance, it was not long ago that pregnancy out of wedlock was considered shocking and shameful. Now we are fighting to keep women from having abortions. Have we accepted the pregnancy out of wedlock part as normal? God forbid. The Bible says your eye affects your heart

(Lamentations 3:51). Jesus warned: *"Take heed what you hear"* (Mark 4:24). What we hear and what we see is affecting our hearts, and it has not always been beneficial. Then, we rationalize, like the rest of society: "That's who I am; I can't do anything about it." Listen, Christians, we should be praying fervently and not allowing these things to continue. We have accepted "garbage" into our hearts and wonder why we are experiencing turmoil, confusion, and warfare in our lives. We have been passive and ignorant. A passive approach to your heart will lead to a heart that is not fixed or established. You must direct your heart to go in the desired direction (God's direction). Your heart is not discretionary; it will accept and produce whatever it is exposed to and is placed in it. The heart is fertile soil and will grow whatever is sown. We need to understand that the heart does not determine what is sown; it just does its job—production, and it does it quickly.

If we are born again, we have a new heart, but we still have the choice of what goes in it. We are instructed to abhor evil (Romans 12:9), abstain from evil (I Thessalonians 5:22), and depart from evil (Psalms 34:14). We cannot use the excuse: "Everybody is doing it." Our society has tried literally to tear our hearts apart. We are to keep our heart with ALL diligence, for out of it flow the issues of life (Proverbs 4:23). If the issue is not producing life, it is producing death: *"I set before you life and death, blessing and cursing: therefore choose life, that both thou and thy seed may live"* (Deuteronomy. 30:19).

When you keep your heart, it not only affects you but also affects those around you (like your children). Stay passive, and the issues flowing out of your heart will not bring life but death. If somebody wants to gossip something into your ear, just say: "Wait, wait, I am leaving, I cannot afford to have my ear become a garbage pail." You might not be very popular for the moment, but you will guard your heart and keep yourself from having to deal with a myriad of problems in your heart. It is easier to deal with a relationship that might be somewhat offended as a result of your action than it will be to try to dig out the roots of the trash sown into your heart. It is imperative we sow life into our hearts. We must be that serious about it. Should somebody start to tell a dirty joke in your presence, say: "Wait, I am going to the bathroom, you tell your joke while I am gone." **Take heed what you hear!** Now, if your thinking, attitudes, and your actions are contrary to the Word of God, and your heart is messed up, the Word of God tells us what to do about it!

James 1:5 says, *"If any of you lack wisdom, let him ask of God, that giveth to all men liberally and upbraideth not; and it shall be given him."* If any of your actions, attitudes, or thoughts are contrary to the Word of God, you lack wisdom. God is not mad at you. He wants you to get it right. James 1: 6-8 goes on to say: *"But let him ask in faith, nothing wavering. For he that wavereth is like a wave of the sea, driven with the wind and tossed. For let not that man think that he shall receive anything of the Lord. A double-minded man is unstable in all his ways."* When your heart is contrary to the Word of God, it is twisted, perverted, and warped.

Note here that James was talking to Christians! Friends, we Christians have become double-minded. We sit in church with one set of attitudes, actions, and thoughts. However, we get home and begin fighting with our mate and screaming at the kids, then sit down to some TV trash. Am I meddling? No, I am trying to save your life. It is time to start walking the *"highway of holiness"* (Isaiah 35:8) and stop existing in the pits of despair and desperation. It is time to stop getting sucked into the world system of fashion, food, and folly. I want you to be able to be a vessel of gold for the Master's use (II Timothy 2:20-21). You cannot act one way one time and the opposite a few minutes later. That is double-minded. You know how to go God's way, but you are thinking the opposite. You may be praising, dancing, shouting, clapping, and singing at church, but ranting, raving, and hollering at someone on the freeway after church. What's wrong with that picture? Teenagers come to church, talk about Jesus, and study the Word, and that is so good. But, when they go to school, do they leave all the church "stuff" behind? Are they drawn in every direction but God's? If you could get their young hearts established and fixed, they could experience the good things of God for the rest of their life.

If we continue to be double-minded and passive about our hearts, we will end up being LUKEWARM, floating to church when we can make it, and staying away if we don't feel like it. Our attitude is that we really cannot make the commitment because we are so busy, and it's hard to come to church twice a week. It is evident there is a problem with that kind of heart. If that is you, action is necessary to do something about it. If it has gone beyond that point, sin has broken out in your life. You know you are wrong and are "scared to death" that somebody else is going to find out. The problem exists in your heart! If sin is constantly cropping up, typically, we try hiding the ugly, diseased, and rotten sin fruit and put it away in a basket. We sure don't want anybody noticing or suspecting our true condition. On the outside, we look like Mr. Johnny Good Christian. However, on the inside, in our hearts, this turmoil, bondage, and garbage are going on. Then we wonder why "Mr. so and so" a "good" Christian is failing, powerless and fruitless. They have been picking the ugly fruit off their old ugly sin tree to keep you from seeing it. What they need to do is to get down to the root and kill the tree.

Some make the determination of not picking a crop of bad fruit anymore, and they cut the tree down. It may appear to be gone, but give it about a year, and a new crop will arrive. You have not been dealing with the **root**. Know that the location of the root is in your heart. Your soulish realm houses the tree and your body the location of the fruit. If you do not deal with the root, you will continue to have crops. When thoughts, attitudes, actions, desires, and passions are contrary to the Word of God, you need to do something about your heart.

No living man can avoid keeping his heart pure if he wants to fellowship and commune with God: *"Out of the heart proceed evil thoughts, murders, adulteries, fornications, thefts, false witnesses, blasphemies: These are the things which defile a man"* (Matthew 15:19, 20). Defile means to become "common." God has put Himself in us through the Holy Spirit so we can walk as supernatural people (I Corinthians 3:16). God has already defeated the devil, putting him under our feet. God has provided us the victory; to be on top; to have no lack; to walk blessed; and to walk in God's best and we must be living in the supernatural realm to do that. But the devil starts planting seeds (thoughts) into our hearts. The seed takes root and up sprouts a baby tree. Soon, fruit is produced on the tree. Common ugly sin-fruit, which brings us out of the supernatural realm as we no longer think the way God thinks. Thinking the way the world thinks brings us down to the common realm.

We have gotten ourselves into a problem because a lot of folks say: "Well, brother, I'm just telling the truth. I am sick". If you say anything contrary to the Word of God, it may be a fact, but it is not "the truth." Because the truth is: *"By His stripes, I was healed..."* (I Peter 2:24). Since you are healed, sickness on you must be a lie. If it is not the truth, why speak it? We need to be speaking like God in accord with His Word. When the devil gets us out of the "Word" realm and not speaking the things out of God's mouth, we start speaking the things as though they appear to our natural eyes. Then, the devil has us down in the common realm and out of the supernatural realm. Then, watch out!

The Common Realm

Christians, filled with the Holy Spirit, have allowed themselves to be defiled. They are walking in the common realm like mere men, and the devil is doing a number on them. All kinds of fear and bondage appear in their lives. They may say: "Bless God, I am trusting the Lord." You are not! If you trusted the Lord, your heart would be fixed and established, and you would not be afraid of evil tidings. Remember, a fixed heart is one being forced to go the direction of the Word of God. Mold your heart. If need be, slap yourself upside the head and say: "Get in here where you belong; you're going this way." If you need to, be tough with yourself. Paul states in Galatians 5:16: *"Walk in the Spirit and you will not fulfill the lusts of the flesh."* A heart fixed and established on the Word of God will be a heart that walks in the Spirit.

A Spirit-controlled heart is one that operates with the Word of God as the final authority. When I discovered this idea (as revelation), I took my stand. When thoughts came, which I knew were not from the Spirit of God, I would say out loud, "Soul, shut up; you are not in control anymore. I am walking in the Spirit, and I am not fulfilling the lust of the flesh." This process has done wonders, even though the thoughts did not always immediately go away. If they didn't leave, I did it again. It is important that you speak out loud. The devil is not omniscient (all-knowing), and he cannot read your mind. So, you need to say it so he can hear it. To deal with your heart, you need to know what the Word of God says so you can utilize it as the weapon it is designed to be. Hosea 4:6 states: *"My people are destroyed for lack of knowledge."* The knowledge referred to in this passage is the Word of God that is sown in your heart. So get in the Word and let the Word get in you. Then, you will have a basis for dealing with your heart.

Your Father God is not "common," and neither are you. So do not allow the world system to "defile" your heart, thus making it "common." The application of the Word of God to your life can cause you to rise above the "common and defiled" category and place you in the position of being *"raised up together and made us sit together in heavenly places in Christ Jesus"* (Ephesians 2:6). Then, with a fixed and established heart (production room), a devastating "fact" will not destroy nor deter you. But you will begin to blast that fact with the "truth" of God's Word. Remember, truth always supersedes any fact because facts are based on circumstances, but the truth is based on God's Word. In Jeremiah 1:12, the Lord states: *"I watch over My Word (truth) to perform **IT.**"* Faith in His truth will alter and change facts.

Christ on the Throne of Your Heart

James 4:8 states: *"Draw nigh to God, and he will draw nigh to you. Cleanse your hands, ye sinners, and purify your hearts, ye double minded."* If we are going to purify our hearts, we must do first things first. Notice the first part of this verse: *"Draw nigh or near to God, and He will draw nigh to you."* It is our responsibility to draw near to Him. There is a beautiful song that starts: "Draw me close to you…" The song has a great melody and wonderful concept but is not in keeping with the Scripture. The scriptural principle is that I must establish the action, and then God will draw close. Remember, when you accept Jesus as Lord, you get a new "want to." It is that new condition of the heart that is how I have any kind of pull in my heart to get close to God.

Remember back to the time when you were not close to God and how you operated primarily on improper concepts of God, most of which was fear-producing (not the reverential kind of fear but the "afraid" kind of fear). You must now make sure you get things in proper order if you want to see the results you desire from Him. You must begin by seeing your heart as God sees it—through the eyes of faith. I believe in teaching that we are the righteousness of God in Christ (II Corinthians 5:21), but I want to tell you that we need to become conscious of sin in our hearts. I am not proposing we develop a sin-consciousness, but rather become cognizant of any time sin or separation from our Father exists. Our spirit is clean and free from the sin nature, but we need to take note any time sin gets even close to our heart—because we are keeping it with all diligence. When evil thoughts come, say: "Get out of here … and stay away". Bring your thoughts into captivity to the obedience of Christ (II Corinthians 10:5).

There is a story about a man that God was using for the great mass exodus of the Jews out of the then iron curtain country of Russia. This man was in a room by himself. The power of God was so strong that he could only lie on the floor, and he remained there for a long time. Another person came into the room but could only stay about ten minutes because that was all of the power of God they could take. That person came into the room, fell, and left by crawling out of the room. Another person came into the room, fell on the floor, and stayed one half of a day before crawling out. This man, while experiencing the presence and power of God, heard Jesus speak plainly and clearly: "I want you to trust me." The man responded: "Lord, I trust you." This conversation was repeated twice more with growing emphasis and urgency. The man opened his eyes and saw that Jesus was standing right in front of him with what appeared to be an ax in His hand. Then, the man screamed because he saw something terrible and ugly: "Lord, what is that?" Jesus said, "That is your heart." The man said, "God, I can't stand it." "I can't stand it either," Jesus said. Jesus then took the ax and laid it to the man's heart, stating: "This is your pride." Jesus laid the ax to the root of pride in the man, and his "old self" literally died in that room. He knew the meaning of Matthew 3:10 experientially: *"The ax is already laid at the root of the trees: therefore every tree which bringeth not forth good fruit is hewn down and cast into the fire."*

Now, this man already knew Jesus as his Messiah. He already knew that Jesus' blood had cleansed him of sin. He knew Jesus as his baptizer in the Holy Spirit, healer, and Lord. Jesus proceeded to go through other things that were in his heart, jealousy, envy, strife, hatred, and bitterness. Each time Jesus exposed something else, the man experienced spiritual pain with physical effects. He could only explain it as though he physically died in that room and was resurrected. When it was over, the man said: "I have never felt so clean and pure."

Let us go back to the garden analogy. I am watering the garden, and water is running down the furrow. The water represents the issues of life. The furrow is fixed and established. A big dirt clod or rock gets in the furrow, and the water begins backing up, and soon it is overflowing the banks.

Now the water is flooding and making a mess of the whole garden. The Lord showed me that those rocks and clods of dirt represent temptations that come into our life. The issues of life are directed and flowing properly, then temptation blocks the stream or flow, and our heart jumps the banks of the direction God has for our life. The rock could be removed by applying the water at greater pressure. But the rock is still in the furrow. The water is washing over it or around it, but the full flow is not there. This happens in our life when we do not take care of the temptation that comes into our lives. Our heart runs out of bounds, and the issues of life flow here and there, and our minds run wild. We may not be tempted to get drunk, commit adultery, or what we consider "big sins," but what about criticism, complaining strife, envy, jealousy, and judgmentalism? We could go further with manipulation and lethargy. Those are temptations. Recognize them as such, and do not try to justify those things. The temptations are plopped right in the path of the water flow in your spiritual furrow. What you are going to do to remove them from your path is your choice.

The Word of God is the tool to deal with temptations. There is more to the Word of God than just saying it is your answer. Acts 15: 8- 9 says: *"And God, which knoweth the hearts, bare them witness, giving them the Holy Spirit, even as he did unto us; And put no difference between us and them, purifying their hearts by faith."* Remember we were just instructed in James to *"purify your hearts, ye double-minded."* At the new birth experience, our hearts are purified by faith. Now James, talking to Christians, said to purify our hearts. At the point of salvation, my will was changed, and Christ sat on the throne of my heart. Now, as a Christian, I can kick Him off the throne of my heart by passive lethargy. I must be aggressive in keeping my heart pure. I must be consistent and assertive to have a pure heart.

How can I get Him back there again? The same way I did when I accepted Him at first, by faith. Remember the Bible states that Christ may dwell in your heart by faith (Ephesians 3:17). To get my heart purified, I go the same route as the sinner-man did. You do not need to get saved again, but you must come to God with a similar attitude of repentance and faith. James 4:9-10 gives us the process: *"Be afflicted, and mourn, and weep; let your laughter be turned to mourning and your joy to heaviness. Humble yourselves in the sight of the Lord, and He shall lift you up."*

We have been too flippant about sin in our lives. We have said: "Oh Praise God, *'there is no condemnation to those who are in Christ Jesus.'"* However, we have forgotten the rest of that verse that says, *"to those that walk not after the flesh, but after the spirit"* (Romans 8:1). To "be afflicted" means to realize one's own misery. This is talking to Christians who have kicked Jesus off the throne of their heart. We are instructed to realize our own misery and the sin and death that we have allowed in our hearts. We are told to weep and mourn. That is called godly sorrow that works repentance. Sin is heavy. Let us not deal with it lightly! Recognize that any desire, attitude, or thought that is contrary to the Word of God is sin and is totally unacceptable to God in our life. Sin disconnects us from the life of God, and we do not want that. Next, make the declaration: "I will not live with sin! But, by laying the ax to the root, I will by the power of the Holy Spirit rid my life of sin and by faith reinstate Jesus Christ to be the Lord of my life and sit on the throne of my heart."

Romans 6:23 says that *"The wages of sin is death...."* We have been living with sin, thinking we could get by with it and nobody would know. We have been good "rotten fruit" pickers. Don't fool yourself. You may never have another person find out about your sin, but you will pay the price. The penalty of sin has been paid for by Jesus and it will be taken care of in your life when you judge the thought, desire or attitude by the Word of God and expel it from your heart. When temptation comes, you must stand against it and say, "No, thank you! Jesus is on the throne of my heart, and I will not give in to it." Jesus must be the Lord of all, or He will not be Lord at all.

Now let us act on the Word of God quickly. Have you come to realize by reading this chapter that your heart is not right? Do you have a desire for a pure heart? Has the Holy Spirit exposed sin in your life? If He has, it is time to deal with it. When we rid our hearts of sin, the heartache of sin will leave. There are so many people, many who are reading this book, that have such hurt and aches in their lives—a result of junk and sin in the heart. Now is the time to do something about it. I encourage you to find a private place where you can be afflicted, weep and mourn. Let godly sorrow work the repentance in you so God can purify your heart. Invite Jesus back on the throne. Cry out to the Lord and get the sin and hurt out of your life and ask God to create in you a clean heart.

Chapter 5

How to Have a Pure Heart

In this book, you will learn the truth about a subject totally misunderstood, neglected, and incorrectly taught in the past: the heart. You may have experienced some tests, trials, and afflictions over what you learned in the last three chapters. Jesus said that when the seed is sown in the heart, satan comes immediately to steal it away (Mark 4:15). Now that truth about your heart has been sown in your life. You must clothe yourself in your spiritual armor (Ephesians 6:13-18). A close friend of mine is a man of God who is a student of God's Word with a deep understanding of God. After hearing me preach the last chapter's message, he had the devil hit him with all kinds of issues. As a result, he had to get his armor latched on tight. The reality is that the devil does not want you to know what your heart is, how to keep it, and how to make it go God's way. The heart is the center and core, the production room of man's senses, emotions, desires, appetites, will, and intellect. If satan can get his thoughts in a man's heart, making it evil and opposed to God's thoughts, he can control the man. If successful, he can alienate us from God's life, God's peace, God's plans, and God's ways.

At this point, you should understand that:

(1) The heart and spirit are not the same.
(2) It is your responsibility to keep your heart.

(3) Your heart was fashioned by God to do His will and respond to God's Word.

(4) Christ can be off the throne of a professing Christian's heart, and

(5) By an act of faith through godly sorrow and repentance, Christ comes back into rulership and lordship on the throne of your heart.

Sin Has Become Too Common

God has impressed me that sin has become too commonplace in the lives of Christians. As believers, we have not been eating the meat of the Word, nor have we exercised our senses to discern good and evil (Hebrews 5:14). Consequently, we have been incrementally drawn into sin: little by little and inch by inch. Every principle that God established works reciprocally in the negative, as well. Line upon line, precept upon precept, works in the spirit realm for us to grow toward God. It also works in the other direction. Please understand that when temptations and problems have crept into our lives, they are like the frog in the pot. Place a frog in a pot of boiling water, and he will jump out. But place a frog in a pot of cold water and slowly heat the water, and the frog will get so accustomed to the water that it will eventually boil him before he realizes what has happened. Unfortunately, that has happened to a lot of the followers of Christ. We become so desensitized to sin that it becomes common to us. Soon we begin to call sin by worldly names such as sickness, phobia, or a habit. It is a sin! Whether it is alcoholism, drug addiction, gossiping, or worry, it is a sin. We do not need fancy names for the thing that comes from the pit of hell. It is the law of sin and death. Sin is anything that disconnects you from the life of your Father God.

If you are riddled with fear, it is a sin because God has not given us a spirit of fear but of power, love, and a sound mind (II Timothy 1:7). Not long ago, one of my church members shared the following story with me. He was on his way to the dentist but was overcome with fear of the dentist. He said that he even sat in the dentist's chair and shook even though the procedure did not hurt. Visiting the dentist was a temptation for him to fear. But if he said: "No, thank you, I do not want the temptation to fear because Christ is on the throne of my heart; I will pass that one by, thank you," then he would not have had the agony of fear. In reality, his fear of the dentist was probably the result of a seed planted in his heart as a child, based on negative words spoken by an adult about the dentist. Consequently, he had a fear tree planted in his heart without knowing how it got there.

Not only do we have to get Christ back on the throne of our heart, but we must also get the ax out and chop off the root. Do not pick the fruit or prune the bush. Get the root out, so it never comes up as a temptation again. Having a plant grow up repeatedly reminds me of a beautiful horseradish plant that was growing right in the middle of my wife's flowerbed. The plant was out of place, so I dug it up and replanted it in another location. However, I did not get all the roots, and it has overrun the very flowers that I was trying to save. The problem was that I did not get the roots. Get the roots out and when you see a little sprout start growing up later, ax it again. When you get the root out, the temptation moves along, and it will not be a temptation. The ax is the Word of God.

Recall, the Gentiles received Jesus as Lord, and God purified their hearts by faith (Acts 15:9). In James, Christians are told to purify their hearts from being double-minded (James 4:8). As we discussed in the last chapter, this purifying of the Christian's heart is done by faith, too. The goal of this chapter is to teach us: "How to have a pure heart." The next step is our responsibility to sanctify the Lord God in our hearts (I Peter 1:15). Sanctify mean to be set apart. God is to be set apart in our heart, on the throne, and in control—calling the shots. We are not going to tell God what to do. **We** have the responsibility to sanctify God in our hearts.

Let us set the stage so we can see "how to have a pure heart." I John.1:9 states: *"If we confess our sins, He is faithful and just to forgive us our sins and to cleanse us from all unrighteousness."* Unrighteousness has something to do with sin. If God cleanses us from all *unrighteousness* after we confess our sins, then the sin relates to unrighteousness. Romans 1:18 states: *"For the wrath of God is revealed from heaven against all ungodliness and unrighteousness of men, who hold the truth in unrighteousness."* The wrath of God is against "unrighteousness." Later in Romans 1:29-30, it states: *"Being filled with all unrighteousness, fornication, wickedness, covetousness, maliciousness; full of envy, murder, debate, deceit, malignity, whisperers, backbiters, haters of God, despiteful, proud, boasters, inventors of evil things, disobedient to parents..."* All the things that are the work of the devil are listed as unrighteousness; connected with sin and with all the works of the devil in men. Romans 6:13 states: *"Neither yield ye your members as instruments of unrighteousness unto sin."* Again, we have unrighteousness and sin connected. II Corinthians 6:14 states: *"Be ye not unequally yoked with unbelievers: for what fellowship has righteousness with unrighteousness?"* Then it is emphatically stated in I John 5:17 that: *"All unrighteousness is sin."*

I tell you this because the unrighteous shall not inherit the Kingdom of God (I Corinthians 6:9), and I want you to inherit the Kingdom of God. Let me continue and make a point not related to the heart that will bless you: *"Let the unrighteous man forsake his thoughts and let him return unto the Lord, and He will have mercy upon him; and to our God, for he will abundantly pardon"* (Isaiah 55:7). Unrighteousness is sin and has something to do with thoughts, according to this passage of scripture. Ephesians 6:16 speaks of the fiery darts of the wicked one. These fiery darts are thoughts thrown at you either through something you heard, saw, or read. But if not dealt with, these thoughts become seeds sown in your heart, and I guarantee your heart will effectively do its job: production and manufacturing.

Zechariah 8:17 reads: *"And, let none of you imagine evil in your hearts against his neighbor."* Imaginations stem from thoughts! Does not the Bible command us to cast down imaginations and every high thing that exalts itself against the knowledge of God and bring into captivity every thought to the obedience of Christ? (II Corinthians 10:5; Author Paraphrase). A thought not dealt with will turn into an imagination—an image you see in your heart.

The unrighteous man is told to forsake his evil thoughts and not to imagine evil in his heart. Evil thoughts are linked to unrighteousness. Jesus told us: *"out of the heart proceed evil thoughts, murders, adulteries, fornications, thefts, false witness, blasphemies"* (Matthew 15:19). Evil is connected with unrighteousness which is connected with sin. All is sin, and evil is part of that unrighteousness.

Whose Report Will You Believe?

Remember the twelve spies who went into Canaan to see the good land God had given Israel (Numbers 13)? They walked into that land, having been told that God had given them the land and delivered the inhabitants into their hands. God told them many times what His plan was, but His words landed on deaf ears and hard hearts. The spies went into Canaan and saw the fruitfulness of the land and the giants that inhabited the area. Ten spies reported: *"We are like grasshoppers in their eyes AND in ours"* (Numbers 13:33). The imagination in their heart was evil because the Word of God stated the ten spies brought an evil report (Numbers 13:32). An evil report is anything that comes out of your mouth that is contrary to the Word of God. Evil is unrighteousness, and unrighteousness is sin, and thoughts coming out of the heart contrary to the Word of God are sin! If you want to tell the truth, speak what God says about your situation. Do not speak the circumstances or declare the fact as the world sees it. Remember, God's words are His thoughts. Hebrews 3:8 states: *"Harden not your hearts, as in the provocation, in the day of temptation in the wilderness."*

The spies that went into Canaan saw the giants and had a temptation placed before them: were they going to believe God, or were they going to believe the giants (what they saw)? Later in Hebrews 3:10-12, referring to the generation of the Israelites in Numbers, it states: *"Wherefore I was grieved with that generation, and said, They do always err **in their heart**, and they have not known my ways. So I sware in my wrath, they shall not enter into my rest. Take heed, brethren, lest there be in any of you an **evil heart of unbelief** in departing from the living God."* Their problem was unbelief in the heart. If you have unbelief, you have an evil heart. An evil heart is unrighteous and sinful. Sin roots in our hearts and needs to be axed out. I am not going to leave you stranded or comfortless. We have identified the problem, and there is a solution. So, we move on to the solution revealing the Word that directs us to the path of correction. Be aware that no one is exempt from this process. So be encouraged in the journey.

The Way Out!

Every Word of God is pure (Proverbs 30:5), but when you do not believe the Word of God you have an evil heart. So we have pure on one side and evil on the other. Therefore, as I sow the Word of God into my heart to root out the evil of unbelief, I will begin to speak that Word. Then as I speak the Word of God against all circumstances, I stay pure. But when I look at the circumstances and say: "Oh, my God, this business is going under, or they will repossess my car," I am looking at sense knowledge (circumstances). I am walking and talking according to the things being produced in a heart that has not yet been purified.

When I talk according to negative conditions and thoughts, I have a heart of unbelief. Subsequently, my actions will be contrary to the Word of God. When your words are evil (contrary to the Word of God), you have regarded or approved iniquity in your heart because *"Out of the abundance of the heart the mouth speaks"* (Matthew 12:34). If I do not do something about the words coming from an evil heart of unbelief,

I regard iniquity in my heart, and the Lord will not hear me (Psalms 66:18). You must take the stand that you will not tolerate anything contrary to the Word of God to even linger for a short time in your heart. You must make the decision to activate the Word of God in your heart to such a degree that your heart becomes so sensitized to anything that does not originate from it. Fill your heart with that kind of action, and you will find your heart having a violent reaction to anything contrary to Father's Word. In your prayer life, have you experienced times when heaven seemed like brass; nothing appeared to be happening and God seemed distant? Check your heart. Are you regarding iniquity in your heart? Are you speaking like the world and circumstances instead of according to the Word of God?

Mark 11:23 says: *"For verily I say unto you, that whosoever shall say unto this mountain, be thou removed, and be thou cast into the sea; and shall not doubt in his heart but shall believe that those things which he saith shall come to pass; he shall have whatsoever he saith."* Out of the abundance of the heart, the mouth speaks. If you believe in your heart, you will speak, and what you speak will come to pass! What kind of mountains could we blow out of our way if we didn't have any doubt in our hearts? We should and must develop an attitude like David's: *"Thy Word have I hid in mine heart, that I might not sin against thee"* (Psalms 119:11). It will take more of the Word than only coming to church on Sunday and mid-week. You must hide the Word in your heart daily because Sunday afternoon through Saturday is when you will be tempted to sin. Do not become satisfied with the diet of the Word you get in church service but develop a ravenous hunger for the Word of God every day and every minute of your life.

"Unto the pure all things are pure: but unto them that are defiled, and unbelieving is nothing pure" (Titus 1:15). What does defiled mean? From the last chapter, we said defiled means to make common or take-down from the supernatural realm and into the common realm. This

scripture links defiled and unbelieving—being in the common realm means that you are out of the believing realm. The believing realm puts you into the supernatural realm. Defiled and unbelieving, nothing is pure. The mind and conscience become defiled, God is denied, and the person becomes disobedient and reprobate (Titus 1:15, 16). Reprobate means unapproved and rejected. Religious practice (man-made rules and regulations) never instills the total position of acceptance in which Jesus has placed you. The man-made religious experience will always place you in a rejected position because you will always have to "earn your way". Thanks to the grace of God, we are in a position that we could <u>never</u> earn. It is a place that only a loving Father could give to undeserving children.

Washed in the Blood of Christ

Matthew 15:8 talks about a people that *"...draweth nigh unto Me with their mouth, and honoreth Me with their lips; but their heart is far from Me."* We do not want to be in that crowd. They are people who dance and shout at church, but when they leave, they cuss and fight and fail to activate the Word at home. They often imagine all kinds of evil thoughts. These are people who hear about how to establish the heart, but instead let it run wild and let strife enter in. This verse says they honor God with their lips and draw nigh to Him with their mouth. They shout their praises to the Lord, but their heart (the production room) is far from Him.

The key to drawing near to God is the blood: *"But now in Christ Jesus ye who sometimes were far off are made nigh by the blood of Christ"* (Ephesians 2:13). By faith we get Christ on the throne of our heart and now by His blood, we are made nigh or near. This passage ties in with James 4:8: *"Draw nigh unto God and He will draw nigh unto you."* The cleansing process is by the blood of Jesus! Hebrews 10:19 reads: *"Having therefore, brethren, boldness to enter into the holiest by the blood of Jesus."* We can walk into the holiest of all, where God dwells, by the blood of Jesus. The blood is the only way into the holiest place! In Hebrews 10:20-22, we read: *"By a new and living way, which he hath consecrated for us, through the veil, that is to say, his flesh; And having an high priest over the house of God; let us draw near with a true heart in full assurance of faith, having our hearts sprinkled from an evil conscience, and our bodies washed with pure water."*

The water he is talking about is the Word of God that will even wash our bodies. We can have our conscience sprinkled clean, cleansed, and purified by His blood. It's the blood of Jesus that is pure enough to cleanse us. Redemption came through His blood (Colossians 1:14). The devil thought he had won by killing Jesus on the cross. The devil didn't know that when those soldiers beat him, scourged him and pierced him, the blood running down His body would provide the victory for every man that placed faith in the precious and holy Blood of Jesus. In Romans 5:1, we read, *"Therefore being justified by faith, we have peace with God through our Lord Jesus Christ."* Verses 8-9 read: *"But God commendeth his love toward us, in that, while we were yet sinners, Christ died for us. Much more then being now justified by his blood, we shall be saved from wrath through him."* We have been justified by the blood of Jesus. Justified means: just-as-if-I had-never-sinned; just as if you were standing there as Adam was on the first day of creation without a hint of sin or defilement. That is the way we stand before God when we take and apply the blood of Jesus to our lives. The key is to believe that His blood cleanses us.

> Romans 3:21-25 states: *"But now the righteousness of God without the law is manifested, being witnessed by the law and the prophets; Even the righteousness of God which is by faith of Jesus Christ unto all and upon all of them that believe, for there is no difference: For all have sinned and come short of the Glory of God; Being justified freely by his grace through the redemption that is in Christ Jesus: Whom God hath set forth to be a propitiation through faith in his blood."*

Salvation is a matter of believing and placing faith in Jesus' blood. It will not come by knowing that you are redeemed, reconciled to God, and am justified by His blood. You must have faith that the blood is doing those things for you, personally and individually. It is the blood of Jesus that will cleanse your wicked, defiled heart out of which come evil thoughts, thefts, and murders. You must take this blood and have such faith in it to redeem you, justify you, and draw you close to God. Have you been feeling far away from God? You can get close! Have faith that the blood of Jesus will draw you right into the holy of holies. John, the Apostle, talking to believers in I John 1:7, said: *"But if we walk in the light, as He is in the light, we have fellowship one with another, and the blood of Jesus Christ, His Son cleanseth us from all sin."*

In summary, remember that all unrighteousness is sin, which is evil. We determined evil is anything contrary to the Word of God or unbelief. To cleanse ourselves, we must have faith in His blood and confess it. For I John 1:9 says: *"If we confess our sins, he is faithful and just to forgive us our sins, and to cleanse us from all unrighteousness."* The cleansing agent is the blood. Confess anything contrary to the Word of God in your life. Weep and mourn and humble yourselves before God and then you will see the cleansing of His blood take place. By faith, we apply the redeeming, justifying, cleansing blood to the heart. So, faith in that blood brings belief. When there is belief in the heart, doubt is gone. When there's no doubt in the heart, you can believe for anything. Without a doubt, unbelief, or unrighteousness, you don't have a heart of unbelief. You don't have any disconnection from God.

Jesus said: *"Blessed are the pure in heart, for they shall see God"* (Matthew 5:8). Do you want to see God? Psalms 24:3-4 states: *"Who shall ascend into the hill of the Lord? Or who shall stand in His holy place? He that hath clean hands, and a pure heart; who hath not lifted up his soul unto vanity, nor sworn deceitfully."* If you want to walk onto the holy hill of the Lord, into the holy of holies, you've got to do it with a pure heart. Get a pure heart by cleansing it with the blood of Jesus and drawing close to God.

Chapter 6

How to Keep your Heart

We discovered in the last chapter that the blood of Jesus cleanses and purifies our hearts as we place faith in the blood. But the cleansing of our hearts will not happen until we are walking in the light. Our ability to walk in the light only happens when Christ is on the throne of our hearts. While we were yet sinners, Christ died for the ungodly (Romans 5:6). You do not get your heart pure and clean, and then Christ comes to sit on the throne of your heart. No, with our consent, Jesus comes to take His place on the throne of our hearts. Then we take His blood and get sin cleansed out of us.

There may be areas in your life where Christ is on the throne, yet there are other areas you must work on. Christ wants to rule the entire kingdom of your heart, not just a part of it. (Mark 12:30). It is a process that happens line upon line, precept upon precept, here a little and there a little. When I was a youngster, I remember singing a song:

"One step at a time, dear Savior, I cannot take any more.

The flesh is so weak and hopeless I know not what is before.

One step at a time, dear Savior, till faith grows stronger in thee,

One step at a time, dear Savior, till hope grows stronger in me,

One step at a time, dear Savior, I am not walking by sight.

Keep step with my soul, dear Savior. I walk by faith in thy might.

One step at a time, dear Savior, oh guard my faltering feet,

Keep hold of my hand, dear Savior, till I and my journey are complete."

Keeping Christ on the throne of your heart is a step-by-step process that involves effort. Paul told Timothy to *"fight the good fight of faith"* (I Timothy 6:12). It is a fight to keep Christ on the throne of your heart and keep your heart purified by the blood of Jesus. It does not happen once, and then you relax. Nor is there a "time out" in the spiritual realm. Take it easy, and you will go downstream with the rest of the folks riding along with the tide of the world, flesh, and sin.

You may desire to get Christ on the throne of your heart and purify your heart, but you are not sure how to do it. Your mouth must get involved in expressing your faith. After Christ is on the throne of your heart, say: "In the name of Jesus, I take the blood of Jesus and apply it to my heart. I take the blood of Jesus and cleanse my heart and purify it." This should be a daily process. Every day in this world, something tries to defile your heart, so you must be consistent and refuse to allow it to happen.

Another way to keep your heart purified by the blood of Jesus is to take communion daily. The Bible says that as often as you take communion, you do it in remembrance of Jesus (I Corinthians 11:25). A significant part of communion has to do with the blood of Jesus, which does the cleansing. Communion sets up a bloodline and the devil cannot cross the bloodline of Jesus. Before the death of Jesus, satan had access to heaven (read the book of Job). After His death and resurrection, Jesus ascended and purified the heavenly utensils of worship with His blood (Hebrews 9:23, 24). The blood of Jesus sends satan running in the opposite direction. If you want to walk in power, start taking communion every day and cleanse yourself with the blood of Jesus.

What is Your Treasure?

The next step to walking in victory is "keeping" your heart. The Bible says: *"Keep your heart with <u>all</u> <u>diligence</u>, for out of <u>it</u> are the issues of life"* (Proverbs 4:23). The understood subject in that verse is "You." "You" keep your heart with all diligence. I want to show you how to keep your heart. Let me remind you, *"A good man out of the good treasure of the heart bringeth forth good things and an evil man out of the evil treasure bringeth forth evil things"* (Matthew 12:35). Jesus is telling us the treasure in the heart will be brought out, be it good or evil. Remember the parable in Luke 15, where a valuable coin was lost. All effort was expended towards finding the coin. The house was swept and cleaned until the coin was found. Why? —because that coin was a treasure. Also, recall Matthew's parable about the pearl of great price. Matthew 13:45, 46 states: *"Again, the kingdom of heaven is like unto a merchant man, seeking goodly pearls: Who, when he had found one pearl of great price, went and sold all that he had, and bought it."*

Jesus gave an example of the merchant that found one pearl of such quality and treasure it did not make any difference what other pearls he saw. None of them looked good after he saw that one. Therefore, he went and sold everything he had to possess that treasure. The Kingdom of God is like that. I raise to you this question: What is your treasure? Is it your house? Your job? Your mate? Yourself? These two parables of Jesus stress the importance of making God, His thoughts and His ways, our treasure, and pursuing them at all costs. That kind of intensity is required, or you will not have a good treasure in your heart. Remember, whatever you treasure in your heart will be brought out. If you do not like what is coming out of your heart and thus your mouth, check your heart. If you do not like what is coming out, change your heart content. So, you need to ask what your greatest treasure is.

Looking at the fourth chapter of Mark, let us review the parable of the sower. In verses 3 through 8, the sower sows on several types of ground. The seed sown is the same, yet different results occur due to varying conditions of the soil. In verse 9, Jesus made a statement I want to highlight: *"He that hath ears to hear, let him hear."* Jesus wanted our attention as He went on to provide His own commentary on the parable of the sower. Jesus' explanation begins in verse 14:

> *"The sower soweth the Word. And these are they by the way side, where the word is sown; but when they have heard it satan cometh immediately and taketh away the word that was sown in their hearts. And these are they likewise which are sown on stony ground; who, when they have heard the word, immediately receive it with gladness; and have no root in themselves, and so endure but for a time: afterward, when affliction or persecution ariseth for the word's sake, immediately they are offended. And these are they which are sown among thorns; such as hear the word; and the cares of this world and the deceitfulness of riches and the lusts of other things enter in, choke the word, and it becometh unfruitful. And these are they which are sown on good ground; such as hear the word, and receive it, and bring forth fruit, some thirty-fold, some sixty, and some an hundred."*

Please notice that God's Word is sown in our heart—the place from where the issues of "Life" flow out. God's Word is not sown in our heads. Although our thinking can overrule God's thinking, God's Word is not sown in our spirit. Consequently, we must understand that the heart is extremely important in our "walk" with God. The Word is sown in our hearts as we hear. (This is more than hearing sounds with our physical ears. It is hearing with the understanding ear.) But five things: persecution, affliction, the cares of the world, the deceitfulness of riches, and lusts for other things can enter our hearts and keep the "God-seed", the "Life-seed" from producing.

Hebrews 3: 12-19 states:

"Take heed brethren, lest there be in any of you an evil heart of unbelief, in departing from the living God. But exhort one another daily, while it is called Today; lest any of you be hardened through the deceitfulness of sin. While it is said, Today if you will hear his voice, harden not your hearts, as in the provocation. For some, when they had heard, did provoke: howbeit not all that came out of Egypt by Moses. But with whom was he grieved forty years? Was it not with them that had sinned, whose carcasses fell in the wilderness? And to whom sware He that they should not enter into His rest, but to them that believed not? So we see that they could not enter in because of unbelief."

The heart is where the Word is sown. The heart can be evil with unbelief, or it can be good with belief. Faith comes by hearing the Word of God (Romans 10:17). So, when we hear the Word of God and receive it, faith will spring up within us that will cause our heart to be a good heart. We are responsible for being stewards over our hearts, not hardening our hearts but receiving the Word.

God Fashioned All Men's Hearts Alike

I was praying one morning, and God said to me: "When I fashioned men's hearts alike, the heart never forgets it. When I touch the heart, it will respond to my touch or respond toward me." Children born into this world, innocent and pure and without sin, have the nature in them that will eventually lead them to sin. But in that child, there is always something drawing them to God. That "something" is God's call for them to worship Him. The call to worship is like the call in geese to fly south for the winter. Because God fashioned man's heart, the touch of God is tugging and pulling (no matter how evil and how hard that heart gets) to bring them out of sin into relationship and fellowship with Himself. If the heart can be evil with unbelief, then belief must be in the heart. Romans 10:9 says: *"That if thou shalt confess with thy mouth the Lord Jesus, and shalt believe in thine heart."* We believe with the heart. Our salvation experience begins with some action **in the heart.** Consequently, out of the abundance of the heart, the mouth speaks (Matthew 12:34). When I receive the Word of God and get it into my heart, belief will be the result, and my heart will be good and have good treasure.

How great it is that God has given us His Word. But God does more than give us His Word. God has given every man **the** measure of faith (Romans 12:3)—the second *"every man"* in this passage means all men everywhere or those afar off. **God** has put His measure of faith in your heart in seed form. It grows when it comes into contact with the Word of God (not just the reading of Scripture, as great as that is, but by the Word that is revealed in your heart). The Scripture is the *Logos* of God, but the *Rhema* is the revealed Word of God. When you plant the *Logos* (written Scripture) in your heart, then the Holy Spirit can bring revelation and understanding to what you have sown. Then you have *Rhema* or the revealed Word of God.

When you were born again, it was by faith after you heard the Word of God; then, as an act of your will, you believed that Word. At that point, the seed of faith in your heart was activated, and salvation (referred to in Mark 4:28 as the "blade") sprang forth. God has put the measure of faith in your heart. Your production room (the heart) has faith in it that lies dormant until you hear and receive the Word of God. Now, you can hear the *Logos* Word of God (the written Scripture) and not receive it. But when you hear the *Rhema* Word of God—the revealed and understood Word—and receive it by believing, then faith grows. The Word is sown, and the heart responds in faith (that measure of faith that God has placed in there), and then Christ can dwell in your heart by faith.

God designed the heart with the <u>measure</u> of faith in it so man could respond to Jesus Christ and Jesus could come in and take His proper place on the throne of man's heart. If we were drawing pictures, we might draw that seed of faith in the shape of a throne in our hearts. The heart responds, Jesus comes and says, "Thank you, I'll sit on this seat of faith in your heart." Let me make just a side note here: God is totally just when He declares in Hebrews 11:6 *"that without faith it is impossible to please God."* He put *"the measure of faith"* in seed form in all men (Romans 12:3) so that all men would have the same opportunity to please Him. All men, even those who have never heard the gospel preached, are without excuse (Romans 1). This passage states that all men can know a divine being because they can look at creation and know there is a God. So, just by observing creation, *"the measure of faith"* can be activated enough to believe in God. All men have the seed of faith in them, so all men can respond to the drawing of God in their hearts.

The Word Keeps Our Heart

It is the Word of God that causes you to keep your heart. The Bible clearly states that the peace of God keeps your heart and mind in Christ Jesus (Philippians 4:7). Also, the peace of God rules in your heart as well (Colossians 3:15). Now follow this sequence: God offers His peace to keep your heart and to rule in your heart. Jesus is the Prince of Peace, and peace will rule in your heart when you let Him rule there. Jesus, the Prince of Peace, is the Word (John 1:1). Consequently, the way to keep your heart is with the Word of God, which will cause peace to rule because the Word **is** the Prince of Peace.

Now, the Bible tells us to keep our heart with all diligence, for out of it come the issues of life (Proverbs 4:23). As we have discussed, that means to guard, attend to, hedge about, protect and take heed to our heart. If you want to build a hedge around your yard to keep the neighbor kids out, you might build one with thorns. They may try to go through it, but once is enough. Next time they will go around the hedge. Likewise, we build the hedge around our hearts with the Word of God. In James 1:3, we read that when we go through various tests and trials, it's the trying of our faith that works patience. The word "patience" here means consistency or constancy. It takes constant and consistent building to get our heart hedged in with our faith. When we do, the devil cannot get to it because there are too many "thorns" in that hedge for him. The good work of patience makes us entire and perfect, lacking nothing (James 1:4). Why? Because faith will get you anything that you want or need.

The Psalmist had the answer as to how the Word of God guards and protects your heart. Psalms 119:11 states: *"Thy word have I hid in my heart, that I might not sin against thee."* We have mentioned the problem earlier in the book. Christians have been deceived by the devil into thinking God will not see our sin. Because of programming through television, newspapers, public schools, and work relationships, we become squeezed into the world's mold. You know the excuse: "Everybody's doing it." If that is your position, your heart is getting hard. If you are involved in sin, you can stop it. God said, *"there is no temptation taken you, but such as is common to man, and with every temptation, God will provide a way of escape..."* (I Corinthians 10:13). God didn't say there is no way to escape, so tolerate it. God said get **OUT** and escape by the way He provides. God is calling our hearts to get purified from sin.

Did you know that young men are sent to the battlefield during wartime, never thinking about getting hit? They think: "Everybody else might, but not me." Christians have developed that same mentality concerning sin. The reason: "I can do this and get by with it." But, when people, even church members involved in sin, visit an anointed church, the sin in them reacts. Sin goes against the nature of God that is in you. It goes against the blood Jesus poured out for you. It goes against the love of God that has been poured out in your heart (Romans 5), and it goes against the life of God and the divine nature that resides **IN** you by the Holy Spirit. The wages of sin is death! Death is separation from the life and fellowship of God. We must somehow get the Word in us to the degree that we understand that sin is deadly.

A Christian who doesn't hate sin cannot purify and put Christ on the throne of their heart. If you do not hate sin, you do not fear the Lord (that is a subject for another time). Stop tolerating sin in your life. Hide God's Word in your heart, and you will not want to sin. You need to appreciate the sacrifice of Jesus, the Lamb. He brought you into fellowship with God through His blood. He made it possible for you to partake of the divine nature and be connected to your Father God again. You are depreciating what Jesus did when you sin. Sin is also a personal offense to Father God—sin hurts God. He loves you that much! Our Father desires close communion with each one of us, but it becomes impossible when sin disconnects us from Him. The key is to get connected and stay connected.

Getting Connected

To get connected and stay connected, we must be careful about the words we speak. Proverbs 6:2 states that we are: *"snared by the words of our mouth."* The words of our mouth cause us to be captured and placed in bondage. With the heart, through the mouth, we either have bondage or freedom. The choice is ours. The question is: "What have we regarded in our hearts? What is the treasure in our hearts? Is it the Word, or is it iniquity?" We cannot regard iniquity in our hearts and expect the Lord to hear us (Psalms 66:19). A casual attitude toward sin is approving sin, and one who approves sin is God's enemy.

Let me give you some scriptures:

"When the law of God is in your heart, your steps shall not slide." (Psalms 37:31)

"God's Word is tried, and the Lord is a buckler (shield and protector) to all who trust in Him." (Psalms 18:30)

"Thy Word is a lamp unto my feet and a light unto my path." (Psalms 119:105)

The Word of God will keep your heart in bounds and on the right path. The Word of God is a lamp unto your feet and a light unto your path. It will keep your heart going down the straight and narrow (fixed and established).

"Great peace have they which love God's law." (Psalms 119:165)

"The Word of God's lips keeps us from the paths of the destroyer." (Psalms 17:3, 4)

Purpose to keep your mouth from transgressing, and you will keep yourself from the evil paths. We do the keeping of our heart and keep the destroyer away by building a hedge around us with the Word of God—a hedge built with the revealed Word of God spoken out of the abundance of the heart. You cannot build a hedge by going an hour a week to church on Sunday morning. You must work on your hedge daily! Let your heart retain God's Word and keep His commandments and live (Proverbs 4:4).

*"Attend to God's words; incline your ear unto His sayings, let them not depart from your eyes; keep them in the midst of thine heart; for they are **life** unto those that find them, and **health** to all their flesh"* (Proverbs 4:20). If you have let the Word depart from your eyes and have not kept it in the center of your production room (Heart), the Word of God will not be life or medicine or health to your flesh. That is the only reason God's Word will not produce for you. If you are having problems, check yourself out—what are you saying?

Now, look at what Jesus was talking about in the parable of the sower. Mark chapter 4:23 says: *"If any man have ears to hear, let him hear. And He said unto them, take heed what ye hear; with what measure ye mete it shall be measured to you; and unto you that hear shall more be given. For he that hath (heard) to him shall be given; and he that hath not (heard), from him shall be taken even that which he hath."* We must place value on what we hear from God's Word. Placing little value on it will cause what understanding we must be taken away. But understand, it is the devil who is the taker, and we make it easy for him by not valuing the Word highly. The more Word we take in, the easier it is to keep it.

Seeing and hearing are the instruments whereby we get the Word into the midst of our hearts. We see it through the eye-gate and hear it through the ear-gate, and it goes into our heart. If you want to hear it well, speak it yourself. It is essential to understand that **your** voice is the authority for your being. You can benefit from preachers and teachers, but if you want the greatest effect, your ears need to hear **your** voice speaking the Word of God. That is why it is so important to have your voice speaking in agreement with God.

To stay connected, we must resist temptations. Snares may be set, but we do not have to err from God's precepts (Psalms 119:110). We must make a stand and tell evildoers to depart because we keep God's commands (Psalms 119:115). This is not a casual or passive attitude. If trouble and anguish have us in their grip, and we delight in God's Word (Psalms 119:143), things will change. To be able to stand, we need some Christian character and backbone developed in us and need to get some steel in our hearts. How do we get that? Make these ten determinations:

1. Determine to recognize sin in your life.
2. Determine to despise it.
3. Determine to repent and go the other way.
4. Determine not to regard sin or approve of it.
5. Determine to get Christ back on the throne of your heart.
6. Determine to purify your heart with the blood of Jesus.
7. Determine to use the Word as the keeper of your heart.

8. Determine to make God's Word the treasure of your heart.
9. Determine to keep your heart whatever the cost.
10. Determine to use the Word as a weapon to protect, defend, and keep your heart.

Make these determinations, and you will be well on your way to being the spiritual giant that you want to be. Instead of being afraid of the devil and always wanting someone to lay hands on you, you will be the one that is looking for someone for whom you can be strong and help. Make these determinations, and you will be the one the devil is afraid to face. You can do it through the Holy Spirit that lives in you. It takes work, and it takes consistency, but you can do it.

Know that when you make that determination, you will have many distractions come and try to steal away your time. Be prepared for this, and then you can avoid it. Remember, we do what we want to do **IF** we want to do it badly enough. If we can see the eternal significance of making these determinations, we can have as much drive to accomplish them as we do to go to work every day. We go to work each day because to provide for ourselves and our loved ones. If we can see the importance of the heart in the same light as the basic instincts of life, then we will have that same drive to do it. You cannot place significance on something if you do not know what it is or how important it is.

Chapter 7

Axing the Roots

Humans are a complex creation of God. All parts of our being are interwoven together. We cannot say there is the heart, there is the spirit, and there is the body. We are all one being, one total person. But there are some things about the heart and its operation that I believe we need to comprehend. In the last chapter, we learned "How to Keep Our heart." Remember, David the Psalmist said, *"I have hid thy Word in my heart that I may not sin against Thee"* (Psalm 119:11). The Lord has confirmed to me that hiding the Word in our hearts is "**the**" key. A lot of us have wanted to stop sinning because it was hurting us or our reputation, or we were afraid someone would find out and think less of us. That is a selfish position. Besides, someone has already found out: Father God.

The motivation for not sinning should be because it hurts the heart of our heavenly Father. Consider not sinning because it makes the blood of Jesus of no effect, and it prevents you from being intimate with the One that loves you more than you can possibly imagine. "That I may not sin against Thee," should be our whole motivation for not sinning. If you believe that sin is disconnecting from your life source: God—why would you want to disconnect? If you understand this, you don't want to do anything that will displease your Father and hinder your fellowship with Him. If you continue to sin, your destiny will be hindered, and you will potentially end your life never fulfilling the very purpose for which you were created.

You must understand that no person is an accident. Perhaps your parents expressed that you were an accident, but not your heavenly Father. Did you know you cannot sin by faith? Without faith, we won't please God (Hebrews 11:6). When you sin, it is not by faith, and God is not pleased. It is always done from a carnal, fleshly, selfish position as an enemy of God (Romans 8). An enemy of God is one position I want to stay far away from. Operating from a carnal position shows a total lack of the fear (reverential awe) of the Lord.

Some of you have been trying to get your heart purified by the blood of Jesus, but it appears something is not working. The blood always works. But you may not have dealt with the ungodly habit patterns or other junk that is in your heart. Before you apply the blood to your heart, you must sweep out some of the trash. Some of you are facing this saying: "Man, I have tried, I have repented, I have wept, and mourned to get Christ back on the throne. Why am I still seeing this junk?" As I mentioned earlier, you have been picking the bad fruit but have not dealt with the underlying problem.

The problem is you have tried to purify your heart with a bunch of roots still in it. Can you get rid of the weeds in your vegetable or flower garden without removing the roots? No, you cannot. I have chopped weeds with a hoe. When you are finished, the garden looks pretty and clean for a while. But then, here comes that ugly weed again. Did you ever try to get rid of a bindweed (wild morning glory)? You can pull the plant up with a very long root. In a few days, it is up again. It is worse than dandelions. I have come to call bindweed the weed from hell because the roots go that deep. Try as I may, I have not been able to get the root, and so it comes back year after year. So, it is with our heart; we have not been getting down to the roots.

The Fruit Reveals the Root

Some of you have been pruning the tree, and you are just getting a larger crop. Some of you have been picking the fruits clean. But wait until next season. You will get a new crop! Matthew 7:15-17 reads: *"Beware of false prophets which come to you in sheep's clothing, but inwardly they are ravening wolves. Ye shall know them by their fruits. Do men gather grapes of thorns, or figs of thistles? Even so, every good tree bringeth forth good fruit, but a corrupt tree bringeth forth evil fruit."* The fruit reveals the root! You cannot have great roots and have rotten fruit. God has established order in the plant kingdom, and nothing violates that order—a corrupt tree brings forth evil fruit. Evil fruit is anything that is contrary to the Word of God. The ten spies in the book of Numbers came back and gave an evil report, speaking contrary to what God had already said to them. They believed what they saw rather than believe what God had said. So they came back with an evil report, speaking out of the abundance of their heart. The fruit in your heart, as evidenced by what you speak, is the reality of the roots in your heart. You cannot get good fruit from a heart that you think is purified if there are still evil roots in the heart. **You must deal with the roots.**

Continuing in Matthew 7:18-23:

> *"A good tree cannot bring forth evil fruit, neither can a corrupt tree, bring forth good fruit. Every tree that bringeth not forth good fruit is hewn down and cast into the fire. Wherefore, by their **fruits**, ye shall know them. Not everyone that says unto me, Lord, Lord, shall enter into the kingdom of heaven, but he that doeth the will of My Father, which is in heaven. Many shall say unto me in that day, Lord, Lord, have we not **prophesied** in thy name? And in thy name have **cast out devils** and in thy name done many **wonderful works?** And then, I will profess unto them, I never **knew** you, depart from Me, ye that work **iniquity**."*

That sounds harsh. These people were saying: "Look at our fruit," but they had some roots that were producing evil fruit. You cannot have good fruit (prophesying, casting out devils, and doing wonderful works) produced from evil roots. Notice the passage, *"I never knew you."* That word, "knew," is the same kind of "knew" that we find in Genesis when it states that Adam "knew" Eve and she conceived and gave birth. What this is referring to is intimacy. Jesus is telling us we can follow instructions and even perform with spiritual gifts without being intimate with Him. But the result will be, *"I never knew you."*

Remember, we talked about people who draw near to God, with their mouths, and their lips honor God, but their hearts are far from Him (Matthew 15:8). Their production room where Christ must be on the throne for the issues of life to flow forth is far from God. There is a problem. Words can be profitable, but words can also be cheap. We have seen people stand up and give their testimony in church, and later we see them at the grocery store cussing at the clerk. These things should not be happening. Sometimes in a spiritual meeting, we see leadership "performing" certain gifts of the Spirit. It all looks good, and even though we are not trying to judge, something inside of us goes "tilt"—we know something is not correct but cannot put a finger on it.

How do Christians get to the place where evil roots are producing bad fruit in their lives?

Hebrews 12:14 reads: *"Follow peace with all men and holiness, without which no man shall see the Lord. Looking diligently, lest any man fail of the grace of God, lest any **root of bitterness** springing up, trouble you and thereby many be defiled."* The Weymouth translation reads: *"A root bearing bitter fruit,"* instead of a *"root of bitterness."*

Many are defiled by the root of bitterness because they have failed to receive the grace of God. Jesus explained: *"Not that which goeth into the mouth defileth a man, but that which cometh out of the mouth, this defileth a man"* (Matthew 15:11). Jesus also said: *"Do not ye yet understand that whatsoever entereth in at the mouth goeth into the belly and is cast out into the draught? But those things which proceed out of the mouth, come forth from the heart, and they defile the man"* (Matthew 15:17, 18). What is in the heart determines whether you are defiled—for out of the heart proceed evil thoughts, murders, adulteries, fornications, thefts, false witnesses, and blasphemies (Matthew 15:19). The thing which defiles a man is the evil that comes out of the mouth—the tongue defiling the whole body (James 3:6).

"Out of the abundance of the heart, the mouth speaks" (Matthew 12:34). When the mouth speaks, the tongue is in operation. Uttering evil words affects the whole body. Concluding this thought, we see that the body is defiled by the tongue, speaking from the abundance of the heart, which is defiled by a root of bitterness resulting from failure to receive the grace of God. All this is the result of thoughts that were not brought into captivity to the obedience of Christ (II Corinthians 10).

Galatians 4:6 states: *"And because ye are sons, God has sent forth the Spirit of His Son into your* hearts, *crying Abba, Father."* This scripture is not out of place. We just concluded from the scriptures that the tongue defiles the whole body because of the things in the heart. Yet God has given us the provision of sending the Spirit of His Son into our heart. Consequently, as a son of God, we no longer must back off from Jehovah, as the Jews did. We have a relationship with God that has taken us out of the realm of slavery and into the realm of sonship. We can cry, "Abba, Father." Slaves were never allowed to cry, "Abba, Father." Abba means "Daddy." Because the Spirit has been put into our hearts, we have the right and the relationship to reach out as a baby grasping His hand and say, "My daddy." Yet, because of "evil" roots in us (born again Spirit-filled Christians), we are not enjoying and experiencing an intimate relationship with "Daddy." Consequently, we live way below our capabilities, privileges, and provisions. We are afraid of God and distant to our "loving Father."

Satan Steals the Word

"The sower sows the Word, the ones along the path are those who have the Word sown in their hearts, but when they hear, satan comes at once and takes away the message that is sown in them. And in the same way the ones sown upon stony ground are those who when they hear the Word, at once receive and accept and welcome it with joy, and they have no real root in themselves and so, they endure for a little while, then when trouble or persecution arises on account of the Word, *they are immediately offended, become displeased, resentful and they stumble and fall away. And the ones sown among the thorns are others who hear the Word and the cares and anxieties of the world and distractions of the age and the pleasure and delight in false glamour and deceitfulness of riches and craving and passionate desire for other things creep in and choke and suffocate the Word and it becomes fruitless."* (Mark 4:14ff; Amplified Bible)

Notice Mark says that undesirable things crept in. That is why we must attend and be on guard over our hearts. If we are not alert, evil things can creep in at the door of our hearts. Evil is subtle. It does not come and dynamite the door down—it creeps in. It sneaks in quietly and unnoticed like a mouse squeezing through a crack in a door.

When satan comes to steal away the Word, he does not come and twist your arm and beat you over the head and say, "Give me the Word"? No, he uses doubt and unbelief. Immediately after you have heard the Word of God, doubt, and unbelief rise up to steal the Word. It is important that you keep your heart with all diligence, or the Word will be stolen away from you. Satan also turns on the heat of affliction and persecution to steal the Word. Then, cares of this world and the deceitfulness of riches and lusts of other things are sent to try and creep into your heart.

There are people who at one time had Christ on the throne of their heart but have missed life's blessings because carnality has crept into their hearts, and they have become lukewarm. Gigantic weeds do not appear overnight in your garden. If I go to my garden early in the morning at the sun's first light, I may see fuzzy little green plants all over the garden—unfortunately, not what I planted. If I go to my garden a few days later and it is full of big weeds, I will determine to get them out of my garden. But, because the weeds creep slowly out of the ground, it's easy to overlook them for a while. We develop the "get them tomorrow" syndrome. The analogy to my garden describes what is happening in our hearts. When we hear anything contrary to the Word of God, we need to act <u>immediately</u>. We cannot afford to let "seed-thoughts" opposed to the Word take root in our hearts. An important point to make here is: you will not and cannot do anything about seed-thoughts that are contrary to the Word of God if you do not know what the Word of God says. That is why we must study it, know it, and hide it in abundance in our hearts.

If you are at the supermarket and sneeze, and someone says, "Oh, you are getting a cold, huh?" That is a seed. Do not let that seed creep in and get planted. Act on that seed. Respond, "I am not getting a cold. I refuse to get a cold because I walk in divine health in the name of Jesus." That's not letting bad seed in your garden. How often do you hear while watching TV: "The flu season is upon us so…"? At that point, you need to declare out loud: "Flu will not come to me because I refuse to have it. I walk in divine health because divine life flows in my veins." That may sound radical, but I will not allow a foreign seed to be planted in my heart.

If you do not **do** something about the "seeds" that are "sown" about daily by everybody you meet, then you will end up with a crop of weeds and then wonder, "Where did that come from." The devil uses any method he can to sow seeds in your heart, and you must always have your guard on duty. *"Guard or keep your heart with **all** diligence for* *out of **it** flow the issues of **life"** (Proverbs 4:23). Guarding your heart will be one of the most important things you ever do as a believer. That is why we believe the statement: Keeping the heart—the key to walking with God.

The Heart Grows the Seed

From Jesus' parable of the sower (Mark 4), we need to understand that the soil is the human heart! When I plant seeds in my garden, the soil has no say-so in what kind of seed is planted. My garden soil makes no evaluation of that seed as to whether it is good or bad. The soil's job is to grow what is planted. When I plant corn, I do not hear the ground saying: "Wait, wait, don't put that corn in here, I want beans here." The heart is the same; it grows whatever is planted. The first thing the seeds produce is roots. It doesn't matter how small a little sprout is; if you pull it out to look at it, you will find a root forming.

The Word of God is a seed (Mark 4), and the word of satan is a seed (Matthew 13). The heart does not determine the quality or kind of seed—the heart grows the seed. Let me digress for a moment. Since God has fashioned all hearts alike (Psalms 33:15), then the heart knows it has a purpose to produce the things of its creator, God. But it cannot determine the seed. It can only grow (and very well, too) what is planted. Imagine the pain and agony the heart must experience when it has to produce evil fruit from evil roots. How tragic. Talk about heartache! The problem with a lot of us is that the seed of satan has been sown in our hearts for years. The seed has rooted too, and we wonder why or how something so bad is so strong in our life.

Many seeds that have taken root in our lives were sown there by family, friends, teachers, etc., none of whom realized what they were doing at the time—and neither did we. So we have had a major problem without knowing the source. If you find yourself in that situation, you need to determine what seeds are of satan. Make no mistake, doubt, unbelief, negativity, and anything contrary to the Word of God is a satan seed. Yes, satan uses people (well-meaning, innocent people) to sow seed in your heart. Take the precautions to build a hedge around your heart, so that evil seed cannot get in.

We know the issues of life flow from our hearts. The term issue means the boundaries or the borders of life. You may wrestle with why you are in bondage in certain areas of life. The seeds of satan have taken root and formed a boundary directing where your life is going. Do you recognize that these satan seed boundaries have kept you from growing in the things of God because the root system is bearing bitter fruit? That seed may have been planted when you were young, and you grew up with resentment and bitterness towards your parents, or you are simply displaying the bitterness and resentment that you saw your parents display. The seed in their heart was transferred to your heart without you even realizing what happened. The sad thing about all the bad seed is this: it will affect your body every time (recall, the heart produces, the soul stores, and the body bears fruit). Deep-seated resentment will cause arthritis. When it attacks the chemical and electrical parts of your body, it can result in multiple sclerosis and many other physical ailments.

Three Steps to Removing the Roots

Now let me give you three steps on "how to get rid of the roots." Matthew 3: 10 says: *"And now, also the ax is laid unto the root of the trees: therefore, every tree which bringeth not forth good fruit, is hewn down and cast into the fire"* (see also Matthew 7:19). According to this passage, we must get the ax to the root and remove the sin plants out of our hearts. Either we ax the root now, or the Lord will take the ax to the root later. I'd rather do it myself. Notice, this passage doesn't say the ax is laid unto the <u>fruit</u> to harvest the crop. It does not say the ax will prune the tree. It does say the ax will get the <u>root</u>. When you get the root, you wield a death blow to it, and the tree stops producing fruit.

Thank God we have been given weapons for warfare that are not carnal (II Corinthians 10:4). These weapons are not something you wield with your hands or even think up with your mind. When things come out of your mouth that defile you, there needs to be warfare. But it is a war we can win. Roots of bitterness, resentment, and anger cause defilement. In fact, all things contrary to God cause war in your heart. Fleshly lusts war against the soul (I Peter 2:11). Your heart has been fashioned by God, not to grow sin/satan seeds, but good/God seeds.

Now, if the tree does not produce good fruit, the ax is laid to the root, and it is cast into the fire (Matthew 3:10). Verse 11 states: *"I indeed baptize with water unto repentance, but he that cometh after me is mightier than I, whose shoes I am not worthy to bear, he shall baptize you with the Holy Spirit and with fire."*

Step One: Be Filled with the Holy Spirit

The **first** step to axing the root is becoming so saturated with the Holy Spirit that the fire of the Holy Spirit will come in and consume the root. You say, "I have been baptized with the Holy Spirit." But how often do you exercise the Holy Spirit within you praying in tongues? It is not enough to pray in tongues when you come to church and sing in the Spirit for a few minutes. If you want to get the ax to the root, pray in tongues at least an hour a day. And if you have heavy-duty roots, just try praying in tongues all day sometimes. If you haven't been baptized with the Holy Spirit, all you need is to be a child of God and ask for it (Luke 11:13). Pray and ask the Lord to totally saturate you with the Holy Spirit.

In Acts 2, it states that you will receive power after the Holy Spirit comes on you. Then one of the first gifts He gives is a heavenly language that Father God understands. It is a language that your mind will not understand, but God understands. Satan is out of the loop and does not understand it and therefore fights it among God's people. So don't be afraid of tongues. It is a precious gift from our Father, so we may pray perfectly. Often, we don't know exactly how or what to pray, so Father has blessed us with a language from heaven so we may pray His perfect will. If this is new to you, get some good books on the subject and read up on it. The little booklet by Kenneth Hagin, "Why Tongues," is an excellent explanation of tongues and the use of this gift.

God has given us all things that pertain unto life and godliness through the knowledge of Jesus Christ (II Peter 1:3). If you want all things that pertain unto life and godliness active in your life, you must go through the knowledge of Jesus Christ (the Door). The knowledge of Him comes from the Word of God. Hebrews 4:12 says: *"For the Word of God is quick, and powerful, and sharper than any two-edged sword, dividing asunder of soul and the spirit, and of the joints and the marrow, the thoughts and the intents of the* heart.*"* The Word of God will make a division between the root and your heart. The Word of God, with the Spirit of God, will chop the root!

Have any of you chopped a root or chopped a big tree down? It would take forever if you took one chop a day or one chop a week? When our spiritual life only consists of coming to church on Sunday, it is like taking the Word of God one chop a week. If somebody hired you to chop down a tree, and you told them, "I'll see you next week," they'd say, "Don't bother. I want the tree out, now". How badly you want those roots out of your life will determine how much of the Word of God that you take daily and apply to that old root. You need to see yourself with the Word of God chopping away at the root. How do you chop? *"Out of the abundance of the heart, the mouth speaks"* (Matthew 12:34).

Step Two: Use the Word of God

If you want to ax the root, the **second** step is to *use* the Word of God. Do not sit around and think it—you must speak it. If satan, through doubt and unbelief, the cares of the world, the deceitfulness of riches and the lusts of other things can uproot the Word of God that is sown in your heart, how much more can you with the power of God (the Word) uproot the devil's seed? You can do it quicker than he can uproot the good seed! You must be as diligent in getting satan's word out of you as satan is to get the Word of God out of you. Satan does not come to you once and say: "Oh, that's not true." He will drive you nuts with repeated lies about the Word of God in your heart until you make a stand and say: "No, I planted it in good soil, and I am fertilizing it." Take the very thing that he tells you is not real and true and exercise it against him. That is how you get your "good" root system down. You will not do it being namby-pamby. Remember to take heed what you hear (Mark 4:24)—if you even listen to his lies, you are in trouble. The Word of God is a two-edged sword. Revelation 1:16, talking about Jesus, said: *"out of His mouth came a two-edged sword."* Glory! We are to be rooted in love (Ephesians 3:17) and in Jesus (Colossians 2:7).

Step Three: Praise

The **third** step to axing the roots is Praise. Enter into praise, and the remainder of that root dissolves away. Psalms 149:6 states: *"Let the high praises of God be in their mouth, and a two-edged sword in their hand."* High praises and the ax go together. With praise in your mouth and an ax in your hand, you can get to those roots. Praise is the fruit of your lips (Hebrews 13:15). So, what if people will overhear you. Do not be ashamed of the gospel or your God! *"MY lips shall utter praise when Thou has taught me Thy statutes"* (Psalms 119:171). When you get the Word of God in you, begin to praise. Praise then releases the power of that Word into the atmosphere, and God can perform the Word. Jeremiah 1:12 states: *"I watch over My Word to perform **IT**."*

God watches over His Word because He will not have it return to Him void and without power. He does not watch over your circumstances to perform them but rather over His Word. That is why you must have His Word coming out of your mouth, so He has something to perform. Find His Word that applies to your circumstance and speak that Word to cover it so God can act on His Word. In the process, you will see your circumstance change. Remember, the facts may be telling you one thing, but the Word is the truth, and truth <u>always</u> supersedes facts and changes them. Truth never changes, but facts do.

When Jehoshaphat (King of Judah) sent his singers out before the army, singing *"Praise ye the Lord"* (II Chronicles 20:22, 23), was used as a weapon. When Paul and Silas were in jail, instead of complaining and moaning about being all locked up in prison, they sang praises unto God (Acts 16:25). It was used as a weapon. It physically shook the place until people (the jailer and his family) were affected as well. We are told to: *"Put on the garment of praise for the spirit of heaviness"* (Isaiah 61:3). Spirit in that passage means life. If the issues of life (out of our heart) are keeping you all bound up, put on the garment of praise, and ax the root of heaviness. In the Old Testament, we recall how the priests wore special robes to minister unto the Lord. We must put on the "garment of praise" if we expect to minister unto the Lord. You enter God's gates with thanksgiving and into His courts with praise (Psalm 100:4). And, in His presence, there is fullness of joy (Psalm 16:11).

Praise suggests surrender or submission, acceptance, and recognition that He is God, and humbleness that you will do what pleases Him. It represents softness as opposed to hardness. Praise suggests that He is on the throne of your heart and puts you in a position to receive fully from God. God is saying to use your weapons. Get the ax to the root. Use the praise as the final blow of the ax on the root, and then you will be able to enter worship.

Your heart will make a complete turn-around when you have axed the roots. So, with 1) The Holy Spirit, 2) The Word, and 3) Praise, you can ax the roots of sin and purify your heart. Then Psalms 57:7 can become a reality: *"My heart is fixed, Oh God, my heart is fixed. I will sing and give praise."* When the roots have been axed, you will not be bothered by reoccurring problems and situations, and you can truly praise God, which will then enter you into true worship. Worship will then get you into an intimate position with your Father where you can hear that "still small voice." Hearing the voice of your precious Heavenly Father will be so wonderful that nothing else from that point on will ever suffice. So, use praise as the weapon it is, and you will see wonderful results.

When Jacob was blessing his sons before he died, he spoke to Judah (whose name means: Praise the Lord), "your hand will be on the neck of your enemy." Praise will put your hand on the neck of your enemy. Remember, there are two times to praise God. One, when you feel like it, and two (and probably more importantly) when you <u>do not</u> feel like it. Just do it.

Chapter 8

Seeds in the Heart

In this chapter, I desire to give you principles about how the Kingdom of God works in our lives and hearts. To do this, we will study the parable of the sower in greater depth.

> *"Hearken; Behold, there went out a sower to sow: And it came to pass, as he sowed, some fell by the way side, and the fowls of the air came and devoured it up. And some fell on stony ground, where it had not much earth; and immediately it sprang up, because it had no depth of earth: But when the sun was up, it was scorched; and because it had no root, it withered away. And some fell among thorns, and the thorns grew up, and choked it, and it yielded no fruit. And other fell on good ground, and did yield fruit that sprang up and increased; and brought forth, some thirty, and some sixty, and some an hundred. And He said unto them, he that hath ears to hear, let him hear."* (Mark 4:3)

Seeds must take root before they grow and produce. It is no different for the "seed" of God's Word. After being planted, the thorn "seeds" immediately come to try and choke the good seed. Now, an important key is "hearing" what Jesus has to say. In the remainder of this parable, the Lord gives His explanation of the story. Mark 4:10 states: *"Now* when He was alone, they that were about him with the twelve asked of him the parable."* Jesus replied to those who asked Him for understanding: *"And he said unto them, unto you (who ask) it is given to know the mystery of the kingdom of God"* (Mark 4:11). You will not find out the mysteries of the Kingdom of God if you don't ask. It was those who asked that got the explanation of the parable. Those who didn't ask were not in this circle to find out the mystery of this parable. In verse 13, Jesus continued: *"And He said unto them, know ye not this parable and how then will ye know all parables?"* Jesus was saying that understanding this parable is the foundation for understanding all parables—He gave them (us) the mystery to the Kingdom of God through it. When they (we) understand this parable, understanding will come to all other parables. I believe that this understanding applies to the heart as well.

Jesus' commentary begins in verse 14: *"The sower soweth the word. And these are they by the way side, where the word is sown; but when they have heard, satan cometh **immediately**, and taketh away the word that was sown in their hearts."* The Word of God is the seed and is sown in the heart (man's production room) by hearing. It's sown in the place out of which flow the issues of life (the heart), and satan comes immediately to steal it. Satan perverts and uses God's principles in reverse or negative fashion, so he sows seed in the heart also. Satan does not create. He only perverts. He can only take what was made for good and pervert it into something evil. For instance, satan only uses temptations that are common to all men (I Corinthians 10:13). He cannot even be creative in tempting us. The same old rotten tricks are used all the time, starting with "seeds" in our hearts. Jesus further explains in verse 16: *"And these are they likewise which are sown on stony ground; who, when they have heard the word, immediately, receive it with gladness; And have no root in themselves, and so endure but for a time; afterward, when affliction or persecution ariseth for the Word's sake, immediately they are offended."*

Growing Roots

For seeds to get roots, they must be watered. I plant seeds in my garden, but if I do not water them, there will be no roots, no plant, and no fruit. That is true for the Word of God also. Some people hear a message and get stirred up, then you never see them again. Try to contact them later, and they tell you to leave them alone. What happened to them is that satan scorched the seed before it could root. They didn't water the seed, and they did not get in a position for anybody else to water it either. Every time someone teaches you from the Bible, they water the Word, if you will receive it. Now, if you expect the entire root to grow up because of someone else watering, you are going to wither. You'd better do some watering yourself: take notes, buy CD's, buy books, read, and listen to them, and re-read the books. As you go over the teaching of the Word again and again, then God starts revealing things to you by His Spirit and applying Holy Spirit water, then the seed sprouts. The root system starts before the seed sprouts up out of the ground. The roots provide support for the plant.

Jesus continues in Mark 4:18: *"And these are they which are sown among thorns such as hear the Word, and the cares of this world, and the deceitfulness of riches, and lusts of other things entering in, choke the Word and it becometh unfruitful."* Now the other two types of ground in this parable have <u>heard</u> the Word. This ground hears the word. Notice that is an ongoing process or continual present tense, not a past tense situation. We are talking about thorns being the cares of this world, the deceitfulness of riches, and the lusts of other things. Every one of us has had seed sown in our hearts by the Word of God among the thorns. But some of us got busy in there and did a weed job.

We must tend the garden of our hearts and not be passive. I am certainly not passive about weeds in my garden at home. I take whatever time I need to get the weeds out. I know that if left unattended, it will not be long before the weeds choke out my vegetable plants. I was cautious to plant my garden seed, and I did not deliberately sow the seeds of my garden among the thorns. The problem was that I could not see the thorn seeds when I was sowing my garden seeds, but when I see the seeds growing, it is obvious the weed seed was there. Just because I could not see it does not mean it was not there. Likewise, with the heart, Word seed sown and watered will force out and uncover the weed seed, but you must be diligent and consistent with the Word to root them out.

To hear the Word must be an ongoing process. The scripture states that *"faith comes by **hearing** the Word of God"* (Romans 10). Hearing is present tense. In the same way that we must continually hear the Word, we must continually get rid of the thorns for the Word of God to produce fruit. Thank God, the seeds of God's Word do not die, but they can lay fallow and not produce. God calls a Christian with that kind of heart lukewarm. These are the people that come to you on the job after you have been there six months and have been witnessing to everybody. They sneak up to you when nobody else is around and say: "I'm a Christian too." They are closet Christians and secret service agents. Why? Because the cares of the world, the deceitfulness of riches, and the lusts of other things are choking them off, and they are not fruitful.

Read this carefully: the seeds from the Kingdom of God do not mix with seeds of this world! They act like oil and water. You cannot hope that the world seeds will just go away; they will not. You **must** take decisive action against the world seeds, or they will choke out the Word of God. God, our Father has given us His Word, but it is up to us individually to use and apply it along with the help of the Holy Spirit who lives **in** us (I Corinthians 3&6).

Jesus continues in Mark 4:20: *"And these are they which are sown on good ground such as hear the Word, and receive it, and bring forth fruit, some thirty-fold, some sixty, and some an hundred."* Good ground also hears the Word on a regular basis. Good ground and thorny ground are both sitting in church every Sunday hearing God's Word. However, thorny ground expects the pastor to water their seed and have it last for the rest of the week. We would not think of eating Sunday dinner and not eating until the following Sunday, but often this is what we do with the Word of God.

The heart operates by having seeds sown in it and produces whatever seed is sown in it because it is very fertile soil. Because the heart rapidly grows whatever is sown in it, it is dangerous to let just any old thing be planted in your heart. You cannot afford yourself the "luxury" of thinking that you can listen to or look at something and not have it affect you. Did you ever look at something just for an instant, not even deliberately, and then battle that image in your brain for weeks to come? A seed was sown in your heart in that instant, and it may take weeks to get rid of it. The heart has fertile soil, and it does not take weeks to have it grow the planted seed. The Psalmist said, *"I will set no wicked thing before my eyes"* (Psalms 101:3). So do not think, "I can handle it," because you cannot. The principle is in motion, and you must use the principle to your advantage, not let the principle take advantage of you.

Being a Doer of the Word

It is our responsibility to get the Word in our hearts, water it, and remove the weeds of care, deceit, and lust. The principles found in the Word will give instruction on how to devour the thorns, deceitfulness of riches (whether you have money or not), and the lust of things. When you apply these principles consistently, you will win the battle. II Corinthians 10:4-5 explains the process. It states that *"the weapons of your warfare are not carnal but mighty through God to the pulling down of strongholds; casting down imaginations, and every high thing that exalts itself against the knowledge of God and bringing into captivity **every** thought to the obedience of Christ."* When a thought comes to you (Ephesians 6 calls it a fiery dart), if you do not immediately bring that thought into captivity to the obedience of Christ, it will form an <u>image</u> (imagination) in your mind. If that image or imagination is not dealt with, it will become a **stronghold** to you (Picture some strong person having a severe grasp of your arm—that is what happens in the heart). It is much easier to deal with a thought than a stronghold because strongholds <u>always</u> have strong roots. Thoughts are not yet rooted. So, get busy on the thoughts immediately!

The planting, watering, rooting, growing, and producing all takes place in your heart. It is important to understand that the heart was made as good soil. It was made to produce quickly and bountifully, but sin brought about another nature that was contrary to the original plan. The different nature—from satan—did not negate the original potency even though he uses the original fertility to produce what he wants to be planted so you won't fulfill your destiny or have any contact with your Father God. Do you see why you are told to *"guard your heart with all diligence..."* (Proverbs 4:23)? Father God knows how He created your heart, and He knows how potent it really is.

Jesus is saying that good ground hears the Word, receives it, and is a doer of the Word also. Doers of the Word bring forth fruit some thirty-fold, some sixty- and some a hundred-fold. In the same manner, as being a producer of the Word (30- 60- 100-fold), conversely, the heart will also produce cares, deceit, lust, etc. If out of the heart flow the issues of life, we can also look at the reverse of having issues of death flow out. The heart is a potent part of us.

As we continue in verse 21, Jesus has not changed the subject, saying: *"And He said unto them, is a candle brought, to be put under a bushel, or under a bed and not to be set on a candlestick?"* God's Word is a lamp unto our feet and a light unto our path (Psalms 119:105). Jesus is talking about the Word sown in our heart, and when received, it will be a light or candle that is not to be hidden under a bushel. The light of God's Word is not sown in our heart to be hidden among thorns but be fruitful (30, 60, and 100-fold) or placed on a stand where it gives light to the whole room. Verse 22 says: *"For there is nothing hid, which shall not be manifested; neither was anything kept secret, but that it should come abroad."*

Jesus is saying that what you sow in your heart is going to come out: *"For out of the abundance of your heart, the mouth speaks"* (Matthew 12:34). That's why the cares of the world, deceitfulness of riches and the lusts of other things keep you from speaking to your neighbor about God. "Too busy" or "too involved" are not excuses I would bring to God. Everything in the heart will be made manifest (and usually at a most inconvenient time). You are going to see it at some time or another. You cannot hide what is in the heart. If it's the Word of God in your heart, it can't be hidden. If lusts of other things are in your heart, that can't be hidden either. If it's the deceitfulness of riches, you can't hide it. Alcohol, drugs, and sex can only mask the vileness in a heart for a very short time, and then soon, it's repeated. *"Be not deceived, God is not mocked; **whatever** a man sows, that is what he will reap"* (Galatians 6:7). In fact, the scripture says the hidden things of darkness will be brought to light (I Corinthians 4).

Seeing and Hearing

Verse 23 and 24 states: *"If any man have ears to hear let him hear. And He said unto them, take heed what you **hear**: with what measure ye mete, it shall be measured to you: and unto you that hear shall more be given."* Sowing in the heart is done by seeing and hearing. Remember the four soil types; the first two "having heard" the Word and the last two "hearing" the Word. We are told to incline our ear unto God's Words and keep them before our eyes (Proverbs 4:20, 21). Everything you hear is trying to sow a seed in your heart. That is why satan has used music so effectively to take hold of the lives of people, especially the youth. You have no defense against music. It will bypass your defense system and get into your heart in a flash. One day I found myself humming the tune from some cigarette commercial. As I caught myself, I thought, "Where did that come from?" It is the little foxes that spoil the vine, so **get your shield up**. Stop looking at and stop hearing garbage, which is anything contrary to the Word. If you are to be fruitful, you must control what your ears are hearing, and your eyes are seeing. If it is out of line with the Word of God, reject it quickly.

Some people in our church once told me that God had done a work in their hearts, removing some seeds that someone had planted in their hearts concerning me. Yes, people had talked negatively about me and planted seeds in their hearts. They had to fight those thorns to get their hearts right. Later, someone planted a seed in them by saying something to them about another church member. They had to fight that thing because it was affecting how they viewed that person. We have all had that experience. That is why we must keep our hearts with all diligence. If somebody on the job comes up and wants to dump on you about the boss, just say, "Wait, I can't handle that, please don't plant that seed in me". If you accept that seed about your boss into your heart, it will open your heart up to receive a whole bunch of other junk. Then there's trouble.

Jesus said: *"Take heed what you hear, for with what measure you mete,"* (the value you place on what you hear) *"it shall be measured back to you and unto you that hear shall more be given."* He is talking about the Word of God. When you place value on the seed of the Word of God and receive it, you establish the furrow of your heart. Then the issues of life can flow out of your heart in a godly direction and have you flowing in the power and might of the Lord instead of always wondering why nothing turns out right for you. But it is also true in the negative. The same principle applies when you place value on the garbage some one's trying to feed you—you will have an abundance of garbage. Respond to someone like I just suggested and watch a door open for further conversation.

Jesus continues in verse 25: *"For he that hath, to him shall be given: and to he that hath not, from him shall be taken even that which he hath."* The one that "hath" is the one that has placed value on God's Word. You place value on the seed of the Word of God planted in your heart by guarding it, keeping it, nourishing it, and watering it. The seed grows, and you have fruit. Then, because you have placed value on it, you will get even more because every seed always produces more than just itself. You will always have more seeds from the original seed. Then, because your soil has been prepared to receive more good seed, you will have more to plant, and the better seed you plant, the bigger crop you get.

Jesus' explanation continues in verse 26: *"So is the Kingdom of God, as if a man should cast seed into the ground; and should sleep and rise night and day, and the seed should spring and grow up, he knoweth not how. For the earth bringeth forth fruit of herself; first the blade, then the ear, after that the full corn in the ear."* Jesus tells us what the entire Kingdom of God is like in operation—remember, the Kingdom of God is within you, in your midst or your heart (Luke 17:21). The entire Kingdom of God works (operates) like casting seed into the ground. Planting seed in our hearts produces either Kingdom of God results or worldly results. The seed we plant is our choice. Are we going to accept worldly seed into our midst, and have it choke off the Kingdom of God? We cannot see or explain how the growth happens. But I guarantee you, when the seed is planted and watered, in your heart; it grows and produces a great harvest.

This is so important for us to operate in the victory Jesus has already obtained for us. Worldly seed sown in our hearts will grow just as good if not better than Word seed. The heart is very fertile and until we have it set and established; it is very accustomed to growing worldly seed. So, it will grow whatever you plant in it. It takes work to get the worldly seed uprooted and cast out of your heart. If we know that, then we will be very cautious of what we see and hear. It is much harder to dig out and uproot than it is to plant. You will be amazed at how fast the worldly seed grows. But thanks to our Father God who has given us the tools to get the wrong seeds out of our hearts.

How do you water the Word seed? By meditating (muttering the Word, speaking to yourself under your breath, thinking about it, always dwelling on it), speaking, hearing, more meditating, seeing, more meditating, and speaking the Word. When you speak, you hear. If you want your seed to really grow, you speak it because your voice is the authority for your being. You need to thank God for the Word working mightily within you every day.

The process of growth for all seed is first the blade, then the ear, then the full corn in the ear. Growth takes time. It doesn't spring up immediately. You may have seed in you from years ago, and when it starts cropping up, you say, "My God, where did that come from?" We cannot sit around watching T.V. about adultery, fornication, and homosexuality and not have seeds planted in us. We need to supervise our children's television viewing as well. Be diligent to plant the Word in your children and water it consistently, and you will not have the normal rebellion you see all around you.

The Small Seed

The Kingdom of God and the seed of the Word of God are seemingly insignificant at the time that they are sown. Mark 4:30 says: *"Whereunto shall we liken the Kingdom of God, or with what comparison shall we compare it? It is like a grain of mustard seed which when it is sown in the earth is less than all the seeds that be in the earth."* Some of you reading this book were born again because somebody somewhere passed you by and on the way said, "God Bless You". That planted a seed in you, which at the time both to you and to them was seemingly insignificant.

We need to see ourselves as a bunch of farmers going about with the awareness that everything that comes out of our mouths is going to plant some sort of seed in somebody. When you go into the supermarket, and things do not go just right, remember that what you say to the new cashier, the lady crowding ahead of you, or the carry-out boy, is a seed. Does it matter if the cashier is slow, or the busy lady is obnoxious, or the carry-out boy is careless? Bless them from a heart of love. Plant the seed in them that "God loves them." Every human being wants to be loved. Once you have planted the seed, they will meditate on it and water it themselves, even though they are not aware from where it came. They may think and say, "You mean God is not mad at me? That person's smile sure seemed sincere and loving. I bet they told me the truth." They will water the seed themselves!

God has put **the** measure of faith in all men (Romans 12). When we give them some Word of God, it is going to activate that seed of faith. As they water that seed, it may result in their being born again. We can go out and sow seeds and may never know the result of it until we stand before God. What a tremendous opportunity we have! Don't ever think the seed that you've been planting is useless, no good, and valueless—when you plant a seed, it grows (Mark 4:32).

Do not say things contrary to what you have sown through prayer! "Why I have been praying for my husband for 20 years, and he is such a jerk." No! You have just poured seed killer on the seed. Do not spray and sterilize the ground with that stuff. Your mouth is the sower to others, but it is the sower to yourself, as well. What you hear then sows it deep. But it grows up, and the thing that was so seemingly insignificant becomes greater than all the herbs and shoots out great branches so that the fowls of the air may lodge under the shadow of it. In concluding this thought, I say, keep your heart with all diligence. Sow the right/correct seeds in your heart so they can take root and grow. Soon you will have a tree that is bigger than others (sinners). They can come and get under the shadow of your tree of the Word of God that is sprouting and fruitful.

I want to encourage those of you who have been sowing God's Word in your heart, and yet life seems overwhelming because you may not have experienced the victory (fruit) of the Word. Mark 4:35 states: *"And the same day when the even was come He said unto them, let us pass over unto the other side."* Jesus, the Word, spoke and set the direction of the boat (Heart) by His words. What happened next? Verse 36, 37 reads: *"And when they had sent away the multitude they took him even as He was in the ship and there were also with Him other little ships, And there arose a great storm of wind, and the waves beat into the ship so that it was now full."*

The storms of life will come. They are trying to ruin your seed, trying to wash your seed out.

If you don't have any root, they can. When the storms of life come, you'd better have the Word on board, or your ship is in trouble. We know the rest of the story. The Word of God won and spoke peace to the storm (Mark 4:39). When the Word of God speaks, He expects it to be carried out. It should be the same in our lives. When we speak the Word of God, we should expect it to be carried out. It will come to pass when we speak if the Word has been allowed to take root and grow. If it is fighting the thorns and thistles, we will have a hard time seeing it come to fulfillment. So, keep on feeding and watering it and rooting out the weeds so it can grow unhindered.

One thing that will keep your heart and mind in Christ Jesus is the peace of God (Philippians 4:7). When you have the Word of God on board (in your heart), you have the "Prince of Peace." When the Prince of Peace says to the storms of life, "Be Still," they are still. When you take the Word of God as seed and plant that seed in your heart, the storms of life come, but they will not win. God says in Jeremiah 5:22: *"Fear ye not me? saith the Lord: Will ye not tremble at my presence, which have placed the sand for the bound of the sea by a perpetual decree, that it cannot pass it: and though the waves thereof toss themselves, yet can they not prevail though they roar, yet they cannot pass over it."*

Plant the seed of the Word of God in your heart and build your heart's banks like a fortress. Let the storms of life roar. The Word that you have planted is like the sand of the sea. It provides the furrow for your heart to flow through. The storms may rage, but they cannot pass over it. They may wash up against it, but you are standing firm. The sands of the sea appear small and insignificant individually. However, when they are put together, they form a barrier whereby the storms and waves of the ocean cannot pass, and the storms must recede! The storms of life will come to you but know this; God has decreed victory and success to those who hear His Word, do His sayings, keep their heart, and apply the blood of Jesus to their life.

Chapter 9

If Your Heart Does Not Condemn You

We have learned that the heart is the very center and core of everything pertaining to life. We also learned that problems in our Christian life occur because of evil in our hearts. Some of you have been taking hold of this teaching and have asked God to turn up the fire in your life to refine your heart! In the smelting of gold, the smelter places the gold ore into extreme heat, and the impurities rise to the top. Next, the smelter removes the impurities and heats the ore further. The process continues until the metal is refined. The smelter needs to know when the ore is refined because if he heats the gold too much or too hot, it will disintegrate. The smelter knows when gold is exactly the right temperature, and all the impurities are removed when he can see his reflection in it.

Jesus wants you to be a vessel of gold unto honor for the Master's use (II Timothy 2:21). By an act of your will (from our heart) you can ask God to turn up the refiner's fire and purge out all the impurities from your heart. He won't do it without your permission and consecration—an act of your will. The Lord showed me our will is like a door. When God approaches and sees our door shut, he knocks. But we are behind the door, and the doorknob is on our side of the door. We must open the door and say: "Yes, come in Lord," (Revelation 3:20).

I have asked questions of myself, my wife, and the Lord about living below our covenant rights and privileges. I have wondered why we don't see the promises of God that we read about in our Covenant Agreement in full manifestation in our lives and why we don't experience the fullness of God in our life. The Bible is not a book of "do's and don'ts." It is our Covenant Agreement with God Almighty. All the promises or provisions God has given to us through Jesus Christ are in the Bible. It is God's revealed will. But, with a Covenant Agreement, there are conditions for each partner. The "if" in the Bible is our part. Fulfilling the promises is God's part. If the promises are not in full manifestation in our lives, the problem is our part. When there is a problem, we need to find out why it exists. Haggai 1:5 states: *"Now, therefore thus saith the Lord of hosts; Consider your ways. Ye have sown much and bring in little; ye eat, but you have not enough; ye drink, but ye are not filled with drink; ye clothe you, but there is none warm; and he that earneth wages earneth wages to put it into a bag with holes."*

Are you facing some battles, problems, or lack? Do you work, and it seems like your paycheck is gone before you get home or to the bank with it? Or is what you read in the Word of God not manifested in your life? If yes, you need to consider your ways. It is not God's way that you need to consider. That is not the problem. Your ways are where the problem is. The problem with a lot of people is that they take their experience and judge the Word of God by their experience. However, we need to take our experience and judge it by the Word of God. The error lies with us. We miss it somewhere when we fall short of God's provisions. God cannot flow His power through a pipe full of mud. I realize this sounds somewhat harsh, but do you want to just be an old clay pot, or do you want to be a vessel of gold? The choice is yours.

Picture yourself going down to the lake to fetch a bucket of water with a container that has holes in it. By the time you run down to the water and get back to the house, it is empty. You do not need more water; you need to plug up the holes. Are you eating and never satisfied? If your heart is saying: "I have given and given and tithed and tithed, but where is the return?" The problem is not God. You have holes in your bag, and it is running out faster than you can fill it up. You read about the promise, *"My God shall supply all your need according to His riches in glory by Christ Jesus"* (Philippians 4:19), but you cannot even pay your bills. You cannot make your house payment; you could not pay your electricity bill last month; you are behind in your car payments. Something is wrong on the inside of you, hindering that promise being fully manifested in your life.

God has revealed the problem and has an answer for seeing His promises fulfilled in your life. Sowing into the Kingdom of God brings a return—not 40 years down the road, either. I remember a year with a new job and five of us in the family to feed. Three were food vacuum cleaners—teenage boys who knew how to eat. They were not fat, just hungry. I started a new job and was totally inexperienced. I worked hard every day but was on a strictly low commission basis. We paid our tithe first on every cent that came in. We did not pay our rent or buy our groceries first—our first check went for the tithe. At the end of the year, all our bills were current, and our debts were paid. My income that year was a lowly $12,000. I have no earthly idea how we paid our bills and bought $500 a month worth of groceries. The point is: our bag did not have a hole in it. In the natural, we should have been so far under it was unbelievable. But we were not! We experienced the promise of sowing and reaping working in our life.

God's Word has the answers! Anytime you find a problem in the world, the Word of God will have a scripture about it. You will have to study, but the answers are in God's Word. If God's promises don't work in your life, it could be because you really don't believe them. If you can't believe the promises, you ultimately must have some problem with the integrity of the Promise Giver. It takes honesty to admit, but that is the underlying problem. Be honest enough with yourself to say that you have a problem believing God. If you are at that place, there is something you can do about it.

> *"Dear children, let us love not with words or tongue, but with actions and in truth. This then is how we know that we belong to the truth, and how we set our hearts at rest in His presence, whenever our hearts condemn us. For God is greater than our hearts and He knows everything. Dear friends, if our hearts do not condemn us we have confidence before God and receive from Him anything we ask because we obey His commands and do what pleases Him."* (I John 3:18; NIV)

God knows what is condemning your heart or what your heart is condemning. He knows what is in your heart. He knows about the sin in your life more than you do. Have you ever had your heart condemn you? What your heart is condemning you about grieves God. God is greater than your heart and does not want sin in you because He knows that sin kills. He knows that sin will destroy the fellowship between you and Him. God knows that sin in your life, that your heart condemns, is causing a strain between the two of you. You cannot draw close to Father God, and consequently, God can't draw you in close to Him since God can't be in the face of sin. It is important to remember that sin is much more than some act that God hates. It is the demonstration of the nature and character of satan himself. It is the destruction of the hold of that nature over us that Jesus came to destroy.

How Your Heart Condemns You

Condemn means to find fault with. God has fashioned all men's hearts alike (Psalms 33:15). Every person has a heart fashioned by God to follow Him. God has placed within us the seed of faith that never leaves

(Romans 12:3). The seed is in there, waiting for somebody to get the Word of God into the heart to germinate it. The Holy Spirit has the seed of faith and the touch of God on our hearts to woo us to God. Your heart really wants to worship Father, but all the worldly junk works at keeping you distanced from Him. That is why God could say that man is without excuse (Romans 2:1). No one will be able to stand before God and say, "I did not know." God fashioned their heart.

> Romans 2:14-15 says: *"When Gentiles who do not have the divine law do instinctively what the law requires they are a law to themselves since they do not have the law. They show that the essential requirements of the law are written in their hearts and are operating there with which their conscience, that's their sense of right and wrong, also bears witness and their moral decisions, their arguments of reason, their condemning or approving thoughts will accuse or perhaps defend and excuse them"* (The Amplified Bible).

Nobody will have an excuse when they stand before God! Every man's heart was fashioned by God in a similar manner. God did not make Oral Roberts or Billy Graham's heart different from yours. God has touched your heart, and it is that touch that wants to respond to God despite the sin that entangles you.

God fashioned, shaped, and formed your production room (the heart) from which the issues of life flow. Because of that, no matter where you are in life, your heart is going to condemn you. That is why you do not have to tell someone they are a sinner. They know it. That, too, is why a backslider cannot look an upright believer in the eye. Their heart condemns them and points out the sin in their lives. Can you see by this the love that God has for mankind? God placed everything that is needed within us to draw us toward Him. He draws, but we must do the responding: *"Draw near to God, and He will draw near to you"* (James 4:8).

The Bible states that even though your heart condemns you, you can rest in God's presence (I John 3:19). We can rest in His presence because we have made the decision to walk in love (I John 3:18). God is love, and love covers a multitude of sins (Proverbs 10:12). Consequently, when you choose to walk in love, you enter a realm where love covers the sin that your heart is condemning you about. That doesn't mean that you don't get rid of (repent and confess) the sin because when you are walking in love, you will be intolerant of sin in your life. When you make that decision to walk in love, you know that you belong to the truth (I John 3:19). Jesus is the truth. We rest in Jesus; we know we are of the truth as we walk in love.

Now, we are ready to understand why the promises of God are not operating in your life. *"Dear friends, if our hearts do not condemn us, we have confidence before God and receive from Him anything we ask as we obey His commands and do what pleases Him"* (I John 3:21, 22). Walking in the truth, resting in God's presence, having a heart that is not condemned, and confidence toward God begins with a decision in your heart to walk in love.

The next step is to ask God to "turn up the refiner's fire." *"But who may abide the day of His coming? And who shall stand when He appeareth? For He is like a refiner's fire, and like a fullers' soap: And He shall sit as a refiner and purifier of silver; and He shall purify the sons of Levi and purge them as gold and silver, that they may offer unto the Lord an offering in righteousness"* (Malachi 3:2, 3). Levi represents the priesthood. We are royal priests (I Peter 2:9). By faith, we are the house of Israel and the kingdom of priests God has always desired (Exodus 19:6). As we begin to walk in love, we will desire to have God's refining fire-heated in our hearts. If we are not walking in love, we will run from the fire. Our prayer must be for God to turn up the fire and purge the sin from our life.

I want the glory of God shining out from me so strong that when I walk down the street, people will be healed and born again. My desire is to build the Kingdom of God, and that requires the Glory of God being manifested; so full of Glory, that as I pass by somebody whose heart is already condemning them, they fall to their knees saying, "Pray for me and help me." God wants that out of every one of us. It won't happen if **your** heart condemns **you**! You must say: "Turn up the fire, God. Get this gold refined. Let's get it so you, God, can see your image in it." Do not wait until tomorrow, do it now! When the fire is hot and the impurities have risen to the top, take the blood of Jesus and cleanse your heart.

Confidence Toward God

When you have made the decision to walk in love and have asked God to turn up the fire, your confidence towards God starts growing. But you will never have confidence in God until you start walking in love. I am talking about walking in love with people who are unlovely. They are God's creation. They are God's loved ones. This will affect the way you respond to and think about God, and the way that you share God with others.

The reason that we have not experienced the promises of God in full manifestation in our lives is that we have not had confidence in God. We have not really believed His promises or His Word. Honestly, we have not really believed Him. We may have intellectually acknowledged His Word, but it hasn't dominated our hearts. Consequently, our heart has condemned us. When our heart doesn't condemn us, we are walking on the highway of love. When we are walking in that love, the promises and life of God will flow from us. Everything you do about God in your life and the consequent promises being manifested is totally dependent upon your confidence toward Him or before Him.

Confidence is complete assurance and boldness. When my wife tells me that she loves me, I have not one ounce of doubt about her love for me. We must be that way with God and His Word. The reason we are not at that point is that our heart has been condemning us because we do not do what it has been fashioned to do. But God (a great phrase in the Bible) is greater than our heart. Your assurance comes from the fact that the Bible was written because of God's love for you. Those promises were motivated by God's special love for you. Now, go out and love your neighbor or your enemy. They are special to God too! If you think that is difficult, Romans 5:5 states that *"the love of God has been poured out in your heart."* You have the equipment to do it—the decision is yours.

The heart was designed to believe God and all His promises, but sin has kept it from doing what it was intended to do: *"Beloved, if our hearts do not condemn us, then we have confidence towards God, and we shall receive from Him **anything** we ask"* (I John 3:22). Unfortunately, certain areas of your heart can be hard. If that is the situation, it will result in your not receiving anything in that area. For instance, I know people who believe in God's provision for their finances, and money is running out of their ears. Yet, they cannot believe God to heal a common cold, even though the same verse of scripture says that God's will is for us to be prosperous and in health (III John 2). The problem is that they do not have confidence in their heart about healing. The financial area is working, but because of doubt, their heart is hard in the healing area, and faith hasn't penetrated the hardness.

To keep your heart from condemning you, make the decision to walk in love—a decision, not a feeling, so just do it. Then, make the decision to get the fire turned up. A lot of people are afraid to say that. But God has your best interests in mind—He wants the best for you more than you do. God also knows what is best for you and will never hurt you. God is not mean to people. In fact, Jeremiah 29:11 says: *"For I know the thoughts I have toward you, says the Lord, thoughts of peace and not evil, to give you an expected end."* That is good news. God may reveal things that appear to be ugly in your heart, but He does so to refine you and get those ugly impurities out. Ultimately, He wants you to be a beautiful vessel of gold for the Masters' use. He does not want to destroy you.

If you have a promise from God's Word and it has not manifested in your life, ask God what is blocking it. When God turns the fire up to where you see it, fall on your face and repent. Clean that heart out, purging it of everything in your life that is not of love, and apply the blood of Jesus after the Word of God blows that ugly thing out of your heart.

Chapter 10

Sanctify God in Your Hearts

In summarizing our study on the heart, so far, you have learned the heart is the production room from where your will, senses, intellect, desires, appetites, and passions stem. You are to keep your heart with all diligence, for out of it are the issues of life (Proverbs 4:23). Whatever direction your life is going today, it is the result of the life (or death) coming out of your heart. You now know that your mouth speaks out of the abundance of your heart (Matthew 12:34). What is coming out of your mouth is a good judging rod for the contents of your heart. Talk of the problem or of the solution comes from the abundance of the heart.

You also learned that when you speak God's Word and meet the conditions of God's covenant, God's provisions are yours. The Word of God in your heart in abundance will cause circumstances and problems in your life to align with God's will. Speaking that way causes the flow to be the "God-kind of life." If you are speaking contrary to God's Word, the course of nature for your life is set in motion by hell (James 3:6). The devil wants your mouth, which has authority on earth, so he can control your life and bring death to you and steal some authority from you. As a spirit-filled, tongue-talking believer, you have yielded some control of your tongue to the Word of God through the Holy Spirit. Praise God for that. You are equipped with a powerful weapon. Jeremiah

1:12 states, *"I (the Lord speaking) watch over My Word to perform it."* Pray in tongues to resist the temptation to speak unbelief and doubt and speak His Word so He will have something to perform.

We have seen in previous chapters that seeds from what you hear or see are sown in the heart. The seeds in your heart can come from the Word of God or from satan. Recall, Peter said to Ananias: *"Why have you let satan put this in your heart?"* (Acts 5:3). Keeping your heart and your potential in God is as great a task as it was for the mighty men of faith, past or present. God fashioned your heart just like theirs.

No man will have an excuse when they stand before God because God has put the seed of faith in each person's heart (Romans 12:3). When any man allows the Word of God into their heart, it contacts that seed of faith, and salvation occurs. After your initial salvation, you can allow sin and ignorance into your heart, so you must then take the Word of God and the blood of Jesus to purify it. In the process of growing and being conformed into the image of Christ, you may have times when sin—that action in the heart—would try to get you totally disconnected from God. But because He has fashioned your heart to go in His direction, your heart will condemn you if your actions try to get it to go in another direction.

God understands your predicament and can override the heart. The scripture states that He is greater than your heart (I John 3:20). So, when your heart condemns you because you are going the wrong way, God is greater and still draws you to Himself. The seed of faith has the power of God in it—the power to draw you to God. It has more power than any depth of sin. Atheists, on their deathbed, breathing their last breath, have cried out to God. For a believer, the sin in your life condemns you, diminishing your confidence towards God and limits the promises of God from manifesting in your life.

It is God's desire to see every promise He ever made to you in total, full manifestation: *"For all the promises of God in Him are yes and amen, unto the glory of God"* (2 Corinthians 1:20). God's desire (Colossians 1:27b) is to see Himself totally and fully manifested in every human being on the face of the earth. God wants the fullness of His glory to manifest in you just like He did with Jesus: *"Christ in you the hope of glory."* When your heart is not condemning you, you can have confidence (complete assurance and boldness) and believe the promises of God with your heart in total agreement with the Word. You cannot separate God from His Word: *"In the beginning was the Word, the Word was with God, and the Word was God"* (John 1:1). When He sees His promises being fully manifested in you, He sees Himself being manifested. We have also learned that we must identify why our heart is condemning us:

The High Places

*"And Jehoshaphat reigned over Judah: he was thirty and five years old when he began to reign, and he reigned twenty and five years in Jerusalem. And his mother's name was Azabah the daughter of Shilhi. And he walked in the way of Asa, his father, and departed not from it, doing that which was right in the sight of the Lord. Howbeit the high places were not taken away. For as yet the people had not **prepared** their hearts unto the God of their fathers."* (II Chronicles 20:31-33)

This passage talks about the idols that the people of God placed and worshiped in the high places. God said: "the high places were not taken away." The reason our hearts have been condemning us is that we have high places in our hearts. We have not prepared our hearts in the sight of the Lord. We cannot have high places or idols existing in our hearts and expect divine life to flow to us and through us.

If there are any areas in your life that do not agree with the Word of God, they are exalting themselves against the knowledge of God. *"The weapons of our warfare are not carnal, but mighty through God to the pulling down of strongholds, casting down imaginations and every high thing that exalts itself against the knowledge of God"* (II Corinthians 10:4,5). Anything *that* exalts itself against the knowledge of God is an idol. God has said: *"You shall have no other gods before me"* (Exodus 20:3). Let's face it (I include myself), we can have idols in our life. It does not have to be a big statue we bow down and kiss every morning—it can be our job, our recreation, our spouse, or any other thing that has the first place in our lives. When your job gets in the way of ministering to the Lord or coming together with the saints or doing the work of God, such as giving to the poor and praying for the sick, it is an idol. You must face up to it and call a sin a sin. Then you can do something about it. But so often, we try to hide it.

If we regard iniquity in our hearts, God will not hear us. We are to pull down every high thing that exalts itself against the knowledge of God. We need God to show us the high places in our hearts, but until we get serious about it, God has to back off. God can only work in the areas of our heart in which we have given Him permission. We all have hard places in our hearts, and it takes the Holy Spirit to reveal them to us. But as we listen and obey, our hearts can get as soft as a baby's face, and the Holy Spirit can move in any way He wants. That is the goal for which we should aim.

Earlier in II Chronicles 11:16, God gives us a principle and a key. Talking about the tribe of Levi, God said: *"And after them out of all the tribes of Israel such as **set their hearts** to seek the Lord God of Israel came to Jerusalem, to sacrifice unto the Lord God of their fathers."* God wants us to set our hearts toward Him, stressing the importance of keeping our hearts with diligence. We cannot let our hearts run out of bounds. We cannot have hearts that wander here and wander there with undisciplined thoughts and minds. God is saying to set your heart to seek the Lord your God.

Do not seek or dwell on the problems. Do not dwell in the world's mess. Do not go swimming in your problems. Problems will always be there trying to get your attention. But make the decision to get your heart in bounds. There will always be injustices in this world, but you can ruin your life and miss your destiny by getting embroiled in trying to "right" every wrong. You must have your heart within the boundaries of the Word of God.

We learned in the last chapter that the Word of God places limitations on our problems as we allow the Word to gird up our hearts. Remember, the Word of God will send the problem away like the waves that approach the seashore. Get out of the ocean of problems and stand on the shore of God's Word and become a doer of the Word. It is not ignoring the problem. It is, however, taking the Word of God, sowing it in your heart and allowing it to come out of your mouth in great abundance, and watching the power of the Word blast the problem away. Keep in mind that the problem is a **fact,** but the Word of God is the **truth:** *"You shall know the truth and the **truth** shall make you free"* (John 8:32). Truth always overrides the fact. Truth is constant, but facts change.

What Does it Mean to Sanctify?

I Peter 3:15 tells us how we get to the point where our hearts won't condemn us. It tells us how to get the issues of life flowing out of us in a profitable manner. We can put an end to our misses and failures. *"But **sanctify** the Lord God in your hearts and be ready always to give an answer to every man that asketh you a reason of the hope that is in you with meekness and fear."*

To sanctify means to set apart and to revere. It means to honor and consider God wholly in your heart. Sanctify means to make God holy or sacred, to purify and consecrate Him in your heart. Religion or traditions will not get you there. It comes through a determination that you are going to set the Lord God as holy in your heart. This is much different from giving mental assent to the Lord—it is total sell-out.

Many of you have developed your concept of God from your relationship with your earthly dad. In most cases, that is a faulty comparison. Consequently, many of you are unwilling to set God apart in your heart and consider Him as holy and reverence Him. When the Bible says to *"Sanctify the Lord God in your hearts,"* it means to develop the fear of God in your heart. We have lost the reverence for God in the body of Christ. It was present in the early part of the 20th century and in the 19th century. Many of our denominations were started by men of God preaching and operating in great power simply because they reverenced God and had developed a fear of God. We have more revelation knowledge than they did, but they respected God as God, the Almighty, the Omnipotent, THE Great Creator.

On the other hand, we have treated God as a "Johnny-on-the-spot" or as a cosmic bellboy that we call when we get into trouble. We have approached God as a benefits machine; we just put the coin in the machine and pull the handle. I have talked with some people within the last year that said: "God has to do this for me." That is not reverencing or honoring God. We must develop a respect for God like David, who said, *"Thy Word have I hid in my heart, that I may not sin against Thee"* (Psalms 119:11). Is it our desire to please God by abstaining from sin? Do we not want to sin because of its effect on God? Do we reverence God so much that we do not want to grieve Him, or are we just afraid of getting caught by somebody?

If you really see sin for what it is—a demonstration of the nature of satan—then you will really want to stay away from it. To do that, you must sanctify God in your heart. Your heart is a holy place for God to dwell where you must honor, revere, and set Him apart. It does not matter what your neighbors or your pastor think, but it does matter what God thinks and feels about it. You need the Lord God sanctified in your heart to such a degree that you will not sin because you would not think of hurting God, the One that gave it all to redeem you and set you free from the bondage of sin. When you arrive at that point, then you will never intentionally hurt your brothers or sisters either. When you love God too much to hurt Him, your brothers and sisters in Christ will experience the same love you have for the Father God.

Praise God for the teachings of righteousness, our position in Christ Jesus, and the authority of the believer. But the abuse of that teaching has sometimes led us to be arrogant with God and mistakenly call it boldness. At times it has produced an arrogant, smart-aleck attitude in believers. That attitude indicates they haven't sanctified God in their heart by considering Him holy and reverencing Him. They have not called their heart a "special place for the Christ." When you realize your heart is a special place for the Almighty God, the King of this universe, the Creator of heaven and earth, the God who died for you, who gave His life for you and defeated satan in the pits of hell, then you will not allow junk (sin) to dwell in your heart.

Your heart is the dwelling place for God, the sanctuary of the Holy Spirit. God dwells right where you live, where the rubber meets the road, and the issues of life are flowing. He dwells in your heart if you let Him. Sanctify Him in your heart, and He will be there to guide every step you take, and you will not have to go through the pits or the garbage dump. See to it that your heart is the place where God dwells. He lives **in** you, not across the street. You cannot hide things in you from Him, who lives in you. You can't hide those ugly words you spoke to your wife or the spiteful way you treated your husband. You can hide it from me or your brothers and sisters, but you can't hide it from God. Why do you want to anyway? It hurts God more than anybody else because every time you sin, you are saying (by that act) that the sacrifice of Jesus didn't do any good. But the problem is that you haven't sanctified God in your heart.

How Do I Know God is Sanctified in my Heart?

Let us look at some scriptures that provide a measuring rod to tell us if God is sanctified in our hearts. *"Purify your hearts, you double-minded"*

(James 4:8). Being double-minded means that one day it is, "Oh, Praise God, everything is glorious, God is so good, I've got the joy of the Lord." But the next day, it is, "Oh, me, where is God?" That double-minded heart has not sanctified the Lord God in it.

Matthew 13:15: *"For this nation's heart has grown gross and their ears heavy and difficult of hearing and their eyes they have tightly closed lest they see and perceive with their eyes and hear and comprehend the sense with their ears and grasp and understand with their heart and turn and I should heal them"* (Amplified). In that passage, the term gross sounds like teen talk. Biblically, gross means fat and dull. Fat speaks of an undisciplined flesh, and dullness is a result of inactivity. Apply this spiritually, and you can see why that nation's heart had grown fat and dull. A heart that is fat and dull has not sanctified the Lord in it.

Matthew chapter 15:8: *"This people draw near to me with their mouth and honor me with their lips, but their heart holds off and is far away from me."* Are you holding off from God—holding Him at arm's length for fear that He might find out something about you? It is too late. He already knows about it. Let God in so He can purify your heart. There are people who draw nigh with their mouth and honor Him with their lips and say all that religious stuff in church and carry out their traditions on Sunday, but their heart is far from God. Why? Because they say one thing at church and do something different in their daily life. That is double-minded and not having the Lord God sanctified in their heart. If your mouth says all the right words, but your life doesn't carry out the right thing, your heart is not sanctified. As the saying goes, "Do not talk the talk if you are not willing to walk the walk."

Concerning faith: *"Whosoever shall say unto this mountain, Be thou removed, and be thou cast into the sea and shall not doubt in his heart, but shall believe that those things which he saith shall come to pass; he shall have whatsoever he saith"* (Mark 11:23). Doubt means to differ or waiver. Have we doubted and differed in our hearts? Did we believe

God one day that the mountain was going to be removed, and the next day we wondered? One day we exclaim: "Praise God, I believe that all my bills are paid," and the next day, it is: "Oh no, I am going to have to file bankruptcy." That is an unsanctified heart.

Hebrews 3:12 is another measuring rod: *"Therefore beware brethren, take care lest there be in anyone of you a wicked, unbelieving heart which refuses to cleave to, trust in and rely on Him, leading you to turn away and desert or stand aloof from the living God"* (Amplified Bible). Is God in total control of your life, or are you standing aloof from Him, not trusting Him to carry out His purpose for you? A wicked and unbelieving heart refuses to cleave to, trust in and rely on the Lord because the Lord God is not sanctified in that heart.

People have rooms in their homes with a particular corner or shelf set apart (sanctified). That area in their home is not for children to play in or touch. As an example, it may be a china cabinet which displays their collection of salt and pepper shakers from all over the world. It is sacred, in a sense, and you respect that area. That is the very kind of approach we should have concerning the Lord God—the Lord God has been <u>sanctified</u> in my heart. My heart is a holy place, made holy and sacred by His very presence. Don't you dare mess with it. You dare not come and unload your garbage in my ears. I'm not talking about those who want to be doers of the Word who come and counsel with their pastor about a problem and respond to the counsel given, but I am talking about those who continue to live in their garbage and problems <u>after</u> "pastor" has given them the Word of God on the matter. If you do not want to do the Word and get out of the mess, keep the problem to yourself.

Problems can become idols in a heart because many people do not really want to get rid of their problem. Their ability to rehearse the problem with anyone who will listen gets them some weird attention. They would rather have negative attention from anyone who will listen than to take the Word of God, grit their teeth, and get the thing conquered. The person that harbors that approach to their problems has a big idol in their heart. They will give you a list as long as your arm to justify their position, but it is obvious they do not have the Lord sanctified in their heart. They may not even know the Lord wants to dwell in their heart.

You must take the Word of God and determine that the Lord God is in your heart and sanctified. Therefore, you will not listen to garbage when someone gossips about a Christian brother or sister. Your response: "Don't you dare bring that garbage into my ears." When shopping at the store and you sneeze and somebody says, "Oh, are you getting a cold again?" If the Lord God is sanctified in your heart, you say, "Oh, no, no, I never catch colds. I walk in the life of God, and divine healing belongs to me." If the Lord God is not sanctified in your heart, you wouldn't even have "guts" enough to say that because you are more concerned about what someone might think about you than you are to hold to the truth of a sanctified heart.

How Do You Sanctify God in Your Heart?

"Sanctify them for yourself, make them holy, by the truth and your word is truth" (John 17:17; Amplified). In that passage, God is saying you can take the Word of God and sanctify the Lord God in your heart with it. The Word of God is your solution, again, IF you become a doer of the Word and not just a hearer only. You become one that says: "Bless God I'm determined. Look out, world. Look out, devil! The Lord God has reverence in my heart, and I'll not sin against Him. You can say what you will. Try and tempt me, but I'll not sin against Him. I will not demonstrate the nature of satan in my life." To sanctify the Lord God in your heart is to place such reverence, respect, and value on the Word that you agree with and practice everything the Word says. Thus, you will be honoring the Lord God (part of sanctification) and sanctifying Him in your hearts.

Without the Word, you would be ignorant. In Ephesians 4:18 (referring to the Gentiles), Paul states: *"Having their understanding darkened, being alienated from the life of God through the ignorance that is in them because of the blindness of their heart."* Blindness, in that verse, means hardness. A hard heart cannot receive the Word of God, which results in ignorance. When you are ignorant, it is impossible to act on what you do not know. You have probably had hard places in some areas of your heart concerning the Word of God. Any area in which you have a problem receiving something as being true suggests a hard place in your heart. It can alienate you from God. That is a tough and difficult place to be.

Receiving the Word of God does affect your heart. That "received" Word will also develop a position for God (a God hold) in your heart. People, who are diligent in studying the Word, meditate in the Word, minister unto the Lord (worship), and pray, have soft hearts. We know what the converse position is. As you read the Word of God, it will affect the position that God holds in your heart because you understand who God is, what He has done for you, and what His plans are for you, and you will respond, "Come on in." Ignorance and misinformation cause us to stay away from God.

Unbelievers cannot give you the right picture of God. Faulty theology and religion (man-made ideas about God) further the spreading of ignorance. For instance, you cannot plant the seed in me (although you might plant it in someone else) that God doesn't heal today. The sower of that seed is an unbeliever in healing, showing their ignorance of the Word on that subject. I am a believer in healing, and I've seen it work. I've seen hands laid on a baby that was dying, and instantly the heart rate changed, and the blood pressure improved so much that the baby was released from the hospital the next day. It is too late to tell me it doesn't work. I laid hands on a lady who had never attended a healing meeting. She did not have any preconceived ideas of how to act. When

I laid hands on her, the power of God was so strong she fell on the floor and got up smiling. When she got up, I asked her what was wrong with her. She told me she had lymphoma cancer and sat through the meeting with pain so bad she could hardly sit, but the pain was all gone! She went back to the doctor for a check-up. The big tumor on her neck started shrinking, and in a matter of three weeks, the doctor dismissed her with no trace of cancer.

If you are a non-believer in healing, you have a hard heart in that area. The Word of God says we were healed by the stripes of Jesus (I Peter 2:24). Any area of God's Word that you have trouble receiving into your heart is an indicator that you have a hard place in your heart. It also tells you that it must be true, or satan wouldn't be working so hard on you to make you disbelieve it. Did you know satan believes that every Word of God is available to us? Why would he work so hard on you to try to get you to disbelieve it? Otherwise, he would leave you alone and let you believe as you wish because it's not going to make a bit of a difference in your life. He believes it so much that it makes him tremble. But if he can get you to believe his lie, he's won.

Sanctify the Lord God in your heart, and your heart will not condemn you, and you will have confidence before God. With assurance and boldness, you will be able to believe all the promises of God, and consequently, you will see all the promises of God manifest in your life. II Corinthians 1:20, *"For all the promises of God in Him are yes and in Him are Amen, unto the glory of God by us."* When I believe the promises of God and act on them as I do believe them, He says, "YES," and then He says, "AMEN," which means SO BE IT. So, you make a decision in your heart to believe His promises, and Father God agrees with you with "yes" and then stamps His declaration on that agreement by stating, "So be it."

In concluding this chapter, I want to give you ten reasons to sanctify the Lord God in your heart.

1. So, Christ may dwell in your heart by faith (Ephesians 3:17).
2. So, the peace of God may keep your heart (Philippians 4:7).
3. So, God's peace may rule in your heart (Colossians 3: 15).
4. So, you may truly hear the cry of your heart; Abba, Father (Daddy) (Galatians 4:6).
5. So, you may fully recognize the light He shined in your heart, which gives the light of the knowledge of the Glory of God (II Corinthians 4:6).
6. So, your heart may be established and unblameable in holiness (I Thessalonians 3:13).
7. So, God can write laws on your heart and be your God (Hebrews 8:10).
8. So, the Lord can direct your heart into the love of God (II Thessalonians 3:5).
9. So, you can love in deeds and truth (I John 3:18).
10. So, you can have confidence, complete assurance, and boldness toward or before God (I John 3:21)

Chapter 11

Results of Sanctifying God in Your Heart

The heart has been a very interesting and beneficial study. I have seen more results from this subject than any other single study that I have undertaken and taught. Many lives have been changed by this teaching, and I thank the Holy Spirit for giving revelation on this subject.

With the foundation we received in the last chapter on sanctifying the Lord God in our heart, we can enter this chapter—"The Results of Sanctifying God in Your Heart." Every time you do something according to God's Word, it produces results. If you gave and claim you never saw any return, there must be some problem because my Father is not a liar. If you do not give motivated by love, it will not profit you (I Corinthians 13:3). You can go so far as to burn your body as a sacrifice, and it will not profit you if it is not done in love. Do things according to the Word of God, and you will always profit from it. It will give you benefits! The Word of God is the declaration of all the covenant benefits from God. That is why we need to apply our minds and heart to it and know it.

I John 3:18 states: *"My little children, let us not love in word, neither in tongue; but in deed and in truth."* Your love should have legs and arms to it. True love does not say, "Oh, I love you, be ye warmed and filled, go your way and get out of my hair." Love says: "Oh, you need some money? Praise God I can give you what I've got." Love shares food with those in need, clothes the naked, putting corresponding actions to what is said. Love performs deeds. I John 3:19 says: *"And, hereby (as we walk in love) we know that we are of the truth, and shall assure our hearts before him. For if our heart condemn us, God is greater than our heart and knoweth all things. Beloved, if our heart condemns us not, then we have **confidence** toward God."*

A condemning heart drains us of confidence. Without confidence, we are not able to believe God's Word. Consequently, we will not see the promises of God manifested in our life. If you say you have been doing the Word and nothing has happened, go back and read the preceding chapter. Confidence towards God produces results, rewards you, and is profitable (Hebrews 10:35). If you have things in your heart that are making you an enemy of God, you will not have confidence in Him. You won't believe when He tells you to get a job so you will have something to give to those that are in need, and then He will supply your need (Ephesians 4:28 and Philippians 4:19). When you believe that, it will change your attitude and performance on your jobs. You will work as unto the Lord and give your very best on the job so you will have something to give to somebody who needs it. When you do that, God says: "I'll supply your need."

Eternity Planted in Your Heart!

It makes no difference if you have never accepted Jesus; it makes no difference if you are the worst sinner in the world; eternity is planted in your heart. It is the divine implantation of purpose for your life that only God can satisfy. You can go every sin-route possible with drugs, booze, or sex and still be empty. You can chase after money, be a workaholic, and pursue any career available and still be high and dry. You absolutely cannot fulfill that divinely implanted purpose of your heart without God. It takes God to satisfy your heart and is futile trying to find a purpose for your life without Him.

When you decide to sanctify the Lord God in your heart is when you know there is a divine purpose in your life. When your will lines up with God's divine purpose, the desires of your heart are in unity and agreement with His will is when you get results. When the desires of your heart are not in line with God's divinely implanted purpose, you can stand on God's Word, confess His Word, pray, and pray but it will not work because it is not God's specific plan for you as an individual. On the other hand, it is God's will for all to be saved, filled with the Holy Spirit, healed, and prosperous. The desires of your heart are planted in your heart from the beginning. It is divine implantation of the purposes that will best suit and benefit you for the fulfillment of God's purpose for being on this earth—the establishment of the Kingdom.

There is a process that you must follow every time you do something with God. Bird hunters don't go hunting, take their gun, point in the air, and shoot, just hoping to hit something. Hunting takes skill obtained through instruction and experience. Let us quit blindly shooting up in the air expecting something to come falling from heaven from God. Zero in on God's will, way, where, when, and how. To follow the process, first and foremost, you must sanctify the Lord God in your heart. God has intended our total being to be entirely in Him. *"In Him we live and move and have our being"* (Acts 17:28). That means my living and moving and being is consistent everywhere I am and whatever I am doing.

Furthermore, you must revere God as God! You must respect God. If you do not have respect, get it. When you do not honor God in your heart, by words and actions contrary to the things of God, you infest your heart. You allow your heart to become infected with evil. *"By reason of use, we have our **senses** exercised to discern good and evil"* (Hebrews 5:14). That means you do not have to be tremendously spiritual to discern good and evil. If your heart is purged by God, your senses in your heart can be trained to know good and evil—you can walk by somebody and sense the evil radiating from them. I can usually look in people's eyes and tell you if they're born again. So, you must make God holy in your heart. If you have sanctified (purified, cleansed, set apart for holy use) the Lord God in your heart, your heart will produce a sanctified life. A sanctified life produces holiness (operating in the nature and character of God). Holiness does not refer to requirements for skirt lengths, shirt color, hairstyle, makeup, and jewelry. While that is outward adorning that will be affected by your holiness (your inward position with God), holiness is an issue of a sanctified life. Holiness is sanctifying the Lord God in your heart, and from that sanctified heart flow the issues of life. From those issues of life comes holiness.

I'm sure you know that what you eat determines the condition of your body. We have heard the statement, "You are what you eat." A person with a high diet of fat is subject to hardening of the arteries and heart disease. In the Word, God tells us to take heed what we hear (Mark 4:24) as our mouth feeds our physical body, so our ears feed our spiritual heart. In the natural, hardening of the arteries comes by overeating fat. To parallel that, eat a spiritual diet of hate, pride, bitterness, resentment, and self-pity; watch soap operas daily or vicariously experience violence on television and see what happens. Christians cannot let these things enter their heart and think the effects will not show up. They can kill your business, marriage, and eventually your life. Pride caused Lucifer to fall from heaven. Jesus said: "I saw him fall to earth like lightning" (Luke 10:18). When lightning strikes the earth, it happens so fast you cannot physically take a picture with an ordinary camera. They take pictures of lightning with light-sensitive film and a readied camera. When the lightning strikes, the shutter automatically goes off. Lucifer fell to the earth that fast when he tried to take over the throne of God. God doesn't fool around with pride. Do not let it in your heart, or it will kill you.

When you live and eat a diet of unforgiveness, doubt, and unbelief, your heart becomes contrary to God. When God is not set apart in your life as holy, purified, and consecrated, spiritual hardening of the heart takes place. It is like a spiritual cancer, a spiritual leukemia running rampant in your veins, and it will kill you. You must throw out the garbage from your life. Sanctify the Lord God in your heart and get confidence towards God, and your sanctified heart will not have anything in it with which to condemn you. God fashioned all men's hearts alike with a divinely implanted purpose that only He can satisfy. If you're doing anything contrary to that purpose, your heart is going to condemn you. Your confidence towards God will be drained, prohibiting the promises of God from coming true in your life.

The Fruit of the Spirit

We have established that a sanctified life flows from a sanctified heart. From that kind of heart, we say: "That I may not sin against thee, Oh God." You need to be intent on God being consecrated and holy in your heart and purpose that the issues of God are going to flow from your heart, and you will do whatever is necessary to keep from sinning against God. With that attitude, you will not desire to sin against your brothers, either.

The high priest in the Old Covenant went into the Holy of Holies once a year, but now everything is different. Now, the Holy of Holies is in your heart. *"Know ye not that your body is the temple of the Holy Spirit"* (I Corinthians 6:19). The temple of God is the holy of holies or where God dwells. God wants to dwell amid your heart. God wants your life flowing with His life so His purposes for you can be fulfilled. When you carry out His divine purpose in your life, contentment comes, and God is pleased because His purposes in your life bring the greatest fulfillment. Leviticus 11:44 and I Peter 1:16 state: *"Be holy, for I am Holy."* The term "holy" means sacred, pure, and blameless. Romans 11:16 reads: *"For if the first fruit be holy, the lump is also holy: and if the root be holy, so will the branches."* When the roots growing in our heart are holy, so are the branches and the fruit on the branches. Good roots come from good seed sown in the heart. Good roots produce good branches, and good BRANCHES produce good fruit.

The manifestation of that holiness is the fruit of the Spirit. The Spirit cannot develop that fruit in your life without holiness, and holiness will not come without a pure heart. So, once again, we see that the heart is central to everything. If the heart is rotten, the fruit of the Spirit cannot flow through it and be manifested. It is like hardening of the arteries—no flow. Since the issues of life flow from the heart, any spiritual truth or action must flow through the heart. If the heart is not cleansed, the spiritual flow cannot happen and that is a dangerous situation.

The fruit of a Christian life is found in Galatians 5:19-23. The first part of that passage is a list of the doings of the flesh; the carnal unsanctified heart—the things you want to avoid.

> *"Now the doings (practices) of the flesh are clear, obvious: they are immorality, impurity, indecency, idolatry, sorcery, enmity, strife, jealousy, anger (ill temper), selfishness, DIVISIONS (dissensions), party spirit (factions, sects with peculiar opinions, heresies) envy, DRUNKENNESS, carousing and the like. I warn you beforehand, just as I did previously, that those who do such things will not inherit the Kingdom of God. But the fruit of the (Holy) Spirit, [the work which His presence within accomplishes] is love, joy (gladness), peace, patience (an even temper, FORBEARANCE), kindness, goodness (benevolence), faithfulness; (meekness, humility) gentleness, self-control (self-restraint, continence). Against such things there is no law."* (Amplified)

We don't have to tolerate any of these activities of the flesh. A sanctified heart will not tolerate them and will work at cleansing the heart of each of them. It is hard work, but it is possible. Why would we want to hang on to the activities of the flesh when the fruit of the Spirit is so much better, even to an unbeliever? The fruit of the Spirit is the character traits of God. If you have not sanctified God in your heart, holiness is not being produced in your heart, and God cannot have His character traits (the fruit of the Spirit) manifested in your life.

The Orange

Let's use an orange as an example of the fruit of the Spirit. The passage does not say "Fruits" plural, but fruit singular. An orange is a fruit. The first fruit of the Spirit is love. Love is like the skin of the orange. The skin peel, meat, and seeds are all the orange. But, the skin is like love. Without the skin, not a single segment (slice) of the orange would ever develop. If the skin is ever injured, part of the orange, and maybe the whole, will not develop. The skin provides the covering or housing to have all those segments (slices) within the orange develop.

Without love, you won't have any joy. The Joy of the Lord is your strength. God **is** holy, and God **is** love, but joy is **of** the Lord. We know in God's presence is FULLNESS of joy (Psalm 16:11). Remember, God **is** love. Inside the orange peel is the FULLNESS of the segment. Inside love is the FULLNESS **of** joy. So, if you want joy in your life, you must spend time in His presence BECAUSE that is where there is FULLNESS. For a segment of our orange to be developed, it must be within the skin.

Peace is mentioned next. Jesus said: *"My peace I leave with you* (John 14:27). Many of you don't have peace in your life. Your life is in a state of turmoil because you haven't sanctified God in your heart. If your heart is not holy, you are not walking in love, and there will be no manifestation of peace in your life. When you don't walk in love, you've gotten outside the orange skin and won't develop peace in your life. But now you know to sanctify God in your life—a deliberate action that doesn't happen by osmosis. The Bible uses the phrase *"peace of God"* in Hebrews 13:20, Colossians 3:15, and Philippians 4:7—peace is of God but is not God.

The next segment is patience or longsuffering. Recall, love suffers long (I Corinthians 13:4). That skin of love keeps the segments together. II Peter 3:15 and II Peter 3:20 mention the longsuffering of our Lord and the longsuffering of God, respectively. If you're not covered with the skin of love, you won't have longsuffering. God is love and therefore suffers long. We suffer long because the fruit of love is being produced in us. Also included in longsuffering is patience. This trait is not tying a knot in the end of a rope and hanging on until something changes. No, patience means consistency. People who are consistent are the ones that you can always count on for whatever is needed. Just make sure your consistency is in line with the application of the Word of God in your life—some people are consistently sad or hopeless or miserable.

The next segment is gentleness—also a slice within the orange that's covered by the skin of love. II Corinthians 10:1 refers to the *"gentleness of Christ."* Without love, you will not be gentle. I am not talking about timidity which comes from fear—gentleness comes out of love. Goodness is the next character trait of God that we will discuss. Many scriptures talk about the goodness of God (Psalm 33:5, Romans 2:4 and 11:22). Again, goodness is developed out of love. You just cannot operate in goodness outside of love. Meekness is the next and often misunderstood fruit. Meekness is not weakness but means humility. Arrogance (pride) is the opposite of meekness. Humility is simply saying about yourself what your Father God says about you; nothing more and nothing less. To some, that may seem to be arrogant but once again, what is the condition of your heart? We have a responsibility not to be moved by what others say. Be moved by His Word over you. Meekness comes from love, and its implied meaning is "teachable." II Corinthians 10:1 mentions the *"meekness of Christ"*. Meekness manifests from a sanctified heart.

Another segment of the Spirit fruit is temperance: the exercise of self-control in your life. Self-control is a manifestation of God being set apart in your heart. Self-control is having your heart flow out of the God-established course and path, going God's direction from a heart that is bound by and propped up by the Word of God. Self-control stems from love, which is produced by holiness. Without self-control, your heart runs out of bounds.

It is a lie that you cannot stop your bad habits. I used to smoke a pipe, but when God told me He was not pleased with that habit, I determined that I would no longer displease the Lord. The Holy Spirit convicted me in my heart when I was standing in a parking lot after a sales meeting at 11:00 p.m. with an expensive pipe in my mouth. I took that pipe and threw it as far as I could. When I got home, I threw all my pipes away, and I have never touched one since, nor have I had the desire to. My ability to break that habit came from God's love for me and my love for Him. I did not want to disappoint Him. So, if you want to break a habit, get saturated in His Word and with His presence through worship. In so doing, you will get engulfed in love, and you will quit your bad habits. Because when you're walking in love, you will have self-control which does not allow bad habits to do the controlling. Love sets up the furrow of your heart, so it doesn't run out of bounds against God's instruction.

I changed the order of the traits of God manifested in us. The King James Bible calls the next one faith. A better translation is Faithfulness. Some of you may not be faithful. You may have joy, and you may have sanctified God in your heart, but, in terms of faithfulness, you have a big gaping hole in your love skin. Unfaithfulness is a sin against God (read Jesus' parable about stewards). The Bible says faithfulness is required of stewards (I Corinthians 4:2). God is faithful (I John 1:9). Man is made in God's image and likeness (Genesis 1:26). If God is faithful, we should be because we are made in His image and likeness. I am faithful to my wife—my wife is faithful to me because we love one another. The last thing in the world I would ever do is be unfaithful to her because of the love we share. Every time there is unfaithfulness in a marriage, there is a hole in the love skin, thus affecting temperance and self-control. Someone in that situation has <u>refined selfishness</u>. They have allowed the skin of love to fall off, and the segments have withered. Consequently, the heart is not sanctified toward God in that area.

When the skin falls off one segment of the orange, it will affect the other areas and eventually ruin the whole fruit. A lot of vegetables and fruits are put into cold storage in food markets. However, the slightest puncture in the skin will cause the whole fruit to deteriorate. But, if it stays intact with no punctures in it, the fruit will keep in cold storage for weeks and never deteriorate. So it is with love. If we allow a puncture, it will deteriorate the whole fruit and cause many areas of our life to be affected though they may seem distantly related to the main problem at hand. *"Now abides faith, hope, and love but the greatest of these is love"* (I Corinthians13).

All these segments of the fruit of the Spirit are encased in love and all are traits that are **of** God. However, God **is** love (I John 4:16). God is the skin that holds all the fruit together. God is not **of** love, and He **is** the totality of love. Without Him, you won't have the other segments inside. So, decide to walk in love. When you decide to walk in love, you have decided to walk in God. How? When you do and speak His Word, then you will see the manifestation of holiness develop from an outgrowth of love. The Lord spoke it to me this way: "No confidence, no love; No love, no sanctifying; No sanctifying, no holiness; No holiness, no fruit; No fruit, and the end result is separation from God."

People of the Vine

We can conclude this study of the heart with Jesus' words in John 15:1, 2: *"I am the true vine and my Father is the husbandman. Every branch that in me that beareth not fruit, He taketh away."* Jesus is not talking to sinners. He is talking to people in the vine. The fruit we bear is love, joy, peace, longsuffering/patience, goodness, kindness, meekness, temperance, and faithfulness. If you are not allowing that fruit to be produced in your life, you cannot draw the life out of the vine. That does not mean you lost your salvation—it means you are placed out of the way, so you don't hurt or hinder anybody else. You should not try to suck the life out of the body that is around you. People who cause trouble in churches (rebellious) get removed and placed out of the way, so they don't hurt the rest of the body.

John 15:2 says, *"Every branch in Me that beareth not fruit He taketh away: and every branch that beareth fruit, He purgeth it, that it bring forth more fruit."* God cleans out the branches so more joy, peace, patience, etc., may come forth. When you bear that fruit, you will be able to go out and tell someone about Jesus and bring that someone into a new life in Jesus. When love, joy, peace, patience, goodness, kindness, meekness, temperance, and faithfulness have developed in you, you will be like a big, ripe, sweet, succulent orange. People will want to taste your fruit. People will be attracted to that love, that joy, that peace and the rest of the fruit that comes from God. They will be able to partake of whatever segment of the fruit they need, and if it is good, they will be back for more.

Pruning is done to produce more fruit. I'm nurturing a grapevine from little sapling seedlings that my dad gave me. They are growing, and after much nurturing, I have a long runner down the fence. Somebody, who had vineyards, told me to annually cut the vines back eight joints from the ground. That was almost my whole vine. But I did it. I pruned my vine. This year I had grapes until my neighbor sprayed his weeds and killed them. I saw the pruning work. That is what God desires in our life. He wants us to produce fruit. God didn't say when we produce a lot of fruit. Then He'll prune us. If we produce any fruit, it tells God we are serious. If we have prepared our heart for the fruit to grow, then God takes that as an invitation to come in to our heart where He can clean all the garbage out so we can produce more. That is what God wants in our lives. John 15:3 tells us how we get purged: *"Now you are clean through the Word which I've spoken unto you."* It is not sickness and disease and calamity that purges us. It is the Word of God.

John 15: 4-7 states: *"Abide in Me and I in you. As the branch cannot bear fruit of itself except it abide in the vine. No more can you, except you abide in Me. I am the vine; you are the branches. He that abideth in Me and I in him, the same bringeth forth much fruit, for without Me you can do nothing. If a man abide not in Me he is cast forth as a branch and is withered, and men gather them and cast them into the fire and they are burned. If you abide in Me and my words abide in you, you shall ask what you will, and it shall be done unto you."*

Ask whatever you will, and it shall be done because you've sanctified the Lord God in your heart, and you're walking a life of holiness. You have confidence towards God, and anything you ask of Him, you believe He is going to do it. He does it because He operates by faith. God trusts us.

John 4: 8-11 states: *"Herein is my Father glorified that you bear much fruit, so shall ye be my disciples. As the Father has loved me, so have I loved you. Continue in my love. If you keep my commandments, you shall abide in me. You shall abide in my love even as I have kept my Father's commandments and abide in His love. These things have I spoken unto you that my joy might remain in you and that your joy might be full."*

Allow me to summarize the process for you:

- Sanctify God in your heart (Set apart, cleanse, purify, for holiness).
- Your heart becomes purified.
- Purifying is laying the ax to the root and uprooting all that garbage (sin).
- Then holiness is produced.
- From holiness, the fruit of the Spirit comes forth.
- Because of love, you have a heart free from condemnation resulting in confidence.
- Then your heart—the production room of your senses, appetites, affections, emotions, desires, passions, and your will—can be fixed and established.
- As you keep your heart with all diligence, the issues of life flow out of it.

Summary

As we have studied the Scriptures concerning the heart, we have distilled the meaning to: "the production room of the soul." The heart is a vital part of our being from which flow the issues of life.

(Prov. 4:23) We have discovered that the keeping of the heart is our responsibility, and we must learn to "fix and establish" it so that we can walk in an intimate relationship with the Lord God. When Christ is on the throne of our heart, we can then operate with a pure heart and be a person that will see God (Matt. 5:8). As we are diligent in keeping our hearts, we will lay the ax to any root that may be growing because of seeds we have allowed to be planted in it. As the scripture says, "As a man thinketh in his heart, SO IS HE" (Prov. 23:7).

We can see the importance of keeping the heart because out of it flow the issues of life. Matthew 12:34 gives us another step by stating that, "for out of the abundance of the heart the mouth speaks."

Words are canisters of power, and whoever is responsible for enacting those words we speak will do so.

Consequently, we must be diligent to guard our thoughts, so improper, ungodly, life-destroying thoughts are not planted in our hearts. The writer of Corinthians gives the instruction in II Cor. 10:5 that we should bring every thought into captivity to the obedience of Christ. By doing that, we will not allow those thoughts to become imaginations which become words spoken that sow seeds in our hearts. If we are diligent in keeping our words pure, we will not have those ungodly, destructive roots in our hearts to which the ax must be used to clean the heart. By obeying the Word, we will make deliberate decisions to sanctify God in our heart, which will please Him, and in so doing, our heart will not condemn us. If our heart does not condemn us, we will be able to walk in a close intimate position with Father God, and then He will have the freedom to flow through us as mightily as He chooses. It will be a glorious journey, and all along the journey, you will be used greatly to establish the Kingdom of God as we prepare for the soon return of the Lord Jesus Christ.

Conclusion

I have assumed that because you have chosen to read this book, that you are born again, and have accepted Jesus Christ as your personal Lord and Savior. However, if you have never made that decision and declaration, let me lead you into that glorious affirmation. Just pray the following out loud."

> *Dear Jehovah God, I choose to believe in my heart that Jesus died for my sin. I now repent and turn from that sin. I choose to believe you raised Jesus from the dead. I now accept Jesus Christ as my Lord and Savior. I confess with my mouth what I believe in my heart. I confess that I am now born again and alive unto you, in Jesus' name. Amen.*

All the information about the heart and what to do with it can be a tough thing to accomplish. But, if you have the power of God come and take up residence in you, then His power is available to you. In Acts 2, we read that when the Holy Spirit comes in, we can walk in power. In I Corinthians 3:16 and 6:19, you see where the Holy Spirit is on planet earth. When He comes to dwell in you, He comes with a load of gifts and fruit for you. Because Father wants to have you in a position of direct communication with Him, the Holy Spirit will give you a new language designed just for the believer. It is so unique that only God understands it (I Corinthians 12). God is so clever because you can pray to Him in His language even if you do not understand it, and in the process, satan cannot understand it either. Therefore, he cannot interfere with the prayer or the answer. This is called tongues. It is a special gift from your Father to you for safety in praying. If you do not speak in tongues, now is the time! Are you "born-again"? Do you want to be baptized with the Holy Spirit and speak in other tongues and receive the power He brings? Praise God!

Luke 11:11 says: *"If a son shall ask bread of any of you that is a father, will he give him a stone? Or if he shall ask for a fish, will he for a fish give him a serpent? Or if he shall ask for an egg, will he offer him a scorpion. If any of you being evil (in comparison to God the Father) know how to give good gifts to your children, how much more shall your heavenly Father give you the Holy Spirit to them that ask Him?"* When you ask the Father for the Holy Spirit, you will get the Holy Spirit. In Acts 2:4, it states: *They were all filled with the Holy Spirit and began to speak in other tongues as the Spirit gave them utterance."* The word utterance means a "prompting".

Now, if I prompted you to say "Hello," you would say "Hello." I did the prompting, and you would do the speaking. It would be your vocal cords and your tongue. I could prompt you to say "Hello," and if you wanted to, you could keep silent. I gave the same prompting as I did before, but you chose not to speak. When the Holy Spirit gives you a prompting, which He will always do, you are the one who is to do the speaking. So, we are going to pray, and I am going to ask you to simply repeat the prayer asking for the Holy Spirit to come into you and take up residence. Then, when we finish praying, I want you to lift your hands and start speaking in that utterance or prompting from the Holy Spirit. It will rise up out of you. It is not "English" or any other language you may have learned. It is not your mind praying. It is your spirit praying (I Corinthians 14:14). You will be talking directly to God (I Corinthians 14:2). Remember, if you ask, you will receive! Pray after me, loud enough to hear your voice:

Father in heaven, I thank you that I am born again. I thank you that I am your son (or daughter). I ask you now to fill me up to overflowing with the Holy Spirit. I thank You, Father, that when I ask You for the Holy Spirit, You will give me the Holy Spirit. I thank You, Father, according to Your Word, that the Holy Spirit will prompt me to speak, and I shall speak in other tongues, and I know I will speak to You. And now I receive the filling of the Holy Spirit. I thank You now for my new tongue with which I can now pray to You, in Jesus' name. Amen.

Now, lift your hands and start speaking in other tongues. Receive the Holy Spirit. I loose your tongue now in Jesus' name, and I command that flow to come forth right now. Thank God for the Holy Spirit. Give God thanks in tongues. You are now equipped to ax the roots from your heart.

Another exciting thing about speaking or praying in tongues is this. The Holy Spirit, being God's Spirit, can only utter God's words. So, when we speak or pray in the Holy Spirit prompted language, we are speaking God's Word. You may not understand it, but He does. In Jeremiah 1:12, God says: *"I watch over my Word to perform it."* What a powerful tool we have from Him. So, at times when I do not know how to pray, the Holy Spirit gives the prompting, and as I give it voice, I can rest assured that I am speaking the perfect will of God, which He can watch over to perform. That is why Jude 20 states that we are built upon our most holy faith, praying in the Holy Spirit. Join that with Romans 10:17: *"So then faith comes by hearing and hearing by the Word of God."* Get this understanding; when I hear the Word of God, my faith will grow, and when I speak that Holy Spirit prompted language, I am hearing the Word of God, which is the perfect part that I need for the occasion. God is so good. Take advantage of all He has provided.

My prayer is that you have been blessed by the reading and doing of the things in this book. I give all the praise, glory, and honor to the Lord Jesus Christ and to the Holy Spirit for bringing me into this revelation. May the rich blessings of the Lord Jesus be upon you as you walk with Him.

*Allan Lewis, **Pastor***

Author Contact Information:

If you would like to have Pastor Lewis speak at your church or gathering, please contact him at the following:

Allan Lewis
880 South Taft St.
Lakewood, Colorado 80228
(303) 284-2157
E-mail: halal@comcast.net

www.ingramcontent.com/pod-product-compliance
Lightning Source LLC
Chambersburg PA
CBHW071852070526
44583CB00016B/1659